THE BOOKS OF

ENOCH

The Book of Enoch (Enoch 1)
The book of the secrets of Enoch (Enoch 2)
The Hebrew book of Enoch (Enoch 3)

CRUX
PRESS

Published by © 2023 Crux Press
2803 Philadelphia Pike
Claymont, DE 19703 United States

ISBN: 978-1-7386005-3-3
ISBN10: 1-7386005-3-X

10 9 8 7 6 5 4 3 2 1

CONTENTS

ENOCH 1

THE BOOK OF ENOCH

ALSO KNOWN AS ETHIOPIAN BOOK OF ENOCH

INTRODUCTION

THE BOOK OF ENOCH (also 1 Enoch) is an ancient Jewish religious work, ascribed to Enoch, the great-grandfather of Noah. It is not regarded as scripture by Jews or any Christian group, apart from the Ethiopian Orthodox Church, which to this day regards it to be canonical.

Western scholars currently assert that its older sections (mainly in the Book of the Watchers) date from about 300 BC and the latest part (Book of Parables) probably was composed at the end of the 1st century BC. However, Ethiopian scholars generally hold that Ge'ez is the language of the original from which the Greek and Aramaic copies were made, pointing out that it is the only language in which the complete text has yet been found.

It is wholly extant only in the Ge'ez language, with Aramaic fragments from the Dead Sea Scrolls and a few Greek and Latin fragments. There is no consensus among Western scholars about the original language: some propose Aramaic, others Hebrew, while the probable thesis according to E. Isaac is that 1 Enoch, as Daniel, was composed partially in Aramaic and partially in Hebrew.

A short section of 1 Enoch (1En1:9) is quoted in the New Testament (Letter of Jude 1:14-15), and there apparently attributed to "Enoch the Seventh from Adam" (1En60:8). It is argued that all the writers of the New Testament were familiar with it and were influenced by it in thought and diction.

The first part of Book of Enoch describes the fall of the Watchers, the angels who fathered the Nephilim. The remainder of the book describes Enoch's visits to Heaven in the form of travels, visions and dreams, and his revelations.

The book consists of five quite distinct major sections (see each section for details):

The Book of the Watchers (1 Enoch 1 – 36)

The Book of Parables of Enoch (1 Enoch 37 – 71) (Also called the Similitudes of Enoch)

The Astronomical Book (1 Enoch 72 – 82) (Also called the Book of the Heavenly

Luminaries or Book of Luminaries.)

The Book of Dream Visions (1 Enoch 83 – 90) (Also called the Book of Dreams)

The Epistle of Enoch (1 Enoch 91 – 108)

The shared view is that these five sections were originally independent works (with different dates of composition), themselves a product of much editorial arrangement, and were only later redacted into what we now call 1 Enoch.

7

This view is now opposed only by a few authors who maintain the literary integrity of the Book of Enoch, one of the most recent (1990) being the Ethiopian Wossenie Yifru. Józef Milik has suggested that the Book of Giants found amongst the Dead Sea Scrolls should be part of the collection, appearing after the Book of Watchers in place of the Book of Parables, but for various reasons Milik's theory has not been widely accepted.

CANONICITY IN JUDAISM

Although evidently widely known at the time of the Development of the Jewish Bible canon, 1Enoch was excluded from both the formal canon of the Tanakh and the typical canon of the Septuagint and therefore also the writings known today as the Apocrypha. One possible reason for Jewish rejection of the book might be the textual nature of several early sections of the book which make use of material from the Torah, for example 1En1 is a midrash of Deuteronomy 33. The content, particularly detailed description of fallen angels, would also be a reason for rejection from the Hebrew canon at this period - as illustrated by the comments of Trypho the Jew when debating with Justin Martyr on this subject. Trypho: "The utterances of God are holy, but your expositions are mere contrivances, as is plain from what has been explained by you; nay, even blasphemies, for you assert that angels sinned and revolted from God." (Dialogue 79)

ENOCH 1

SECTION I.
CHAPTERS I-XXXVI
BOOK OF THE WATCHERS

1.1 These are the words of the blessing of Enoch; according to which he blessed the chosen and righteous who must be present on the day of distress, which is appointed, for the removal of all the wicked and impious.

1.2 And Enoch began his story and said:
-

There was a righteous man whose eyes were opened by the Lord, and he saw a Holy Vision in the Heavens, which the Angels showed to me. And I heard everything from them, and I understood what I saw: but not for this generation, but for a distant generation that will come.

1.3 Concerning the Chosen I spoke; and I uttered a parable concerning them: The Holy and Great One will come out of his dwelling.

1.4 And the Eternal God will tread from there upon Mount Sinai, and he will appear with his Host, and will appear in the strength of his power from Heaven.

1.5 And all will be afraid, and the Watchers will shake, and fear and great trembling will seize them, up to the ends of the earth.

1.6 And the high mountains will be shaken; and the high hills will be laid low and will melt like wax in a flame.

1.7 And the earth will sink, and everything that is on the earth will be destroyed, and there will be judgment upon all, and upon all the righteous.

1.8 But for the righteous: He will make peace, and He will keep safe the Chosen, and mercy will be upon them. They will all belong to God, and will prosper and be blessed, and the light of God will shine on them.

1.9 And behold! He comes with ten thousand Holy Ones; to execute judgment upon them and to destroy the impious, and to contend with all flesh concerning everything that the sinners and the impious have done and wrought against Him.

2.1 Contemplate all the events in the sky; how the lights in the sky do not change their courses, how each rises and sets in order, each at its proper time, and they do not transgress their law.

2.2 Consider the earth and understand from the work that is done upon it, from the beginning to the end, that no work of God changes as it becomes manifest.

2.3 Consider the summer and the winter; how the whole earth is full of water and the clouds and dew and rain rest upon it.

3.1 Contemplate and see how all the trees appear withered and all their leaves are stripped - except for the fourteen trees, which are not stripped, which remain with the old leaves until the new come after two or three years.

4.1 And, again, contemplate the days

of summer; how at its beginning the Sun is above it. You seek shelter and shade because of the heat of the Sun and the earth burns with scorching heat, and you cannot tread upon the earth or upon a rock, because of its heat.

5.1 Contemplate how the trees are covered with green leaves and bear fruit. And understand, in respect of everything, and perceive how He Who Lives Forever made all these things for you.

5.2 And how His works are before Him in each succeeding year, and all His works serve Him and do not change; but as God has decreed - so everything is done.

5.3 And consider how the seas and rivers together complete their tasks.

5.4 But you have not persevered in, nor observed, the Law of the Lord. But you have transgressed and have spoken proud and hard words with your unclean mouth against his majesty. You hard of heart! You will not have peace!

5.5 And because of this you will curse your days, and the years of your life you will destroy. And the eternal curse will increase and you will not receive mercy.

5.6 In those days, you will transform your name into an eternal curse to all the righteous. And they will curse you sinners forever.

5.7 For the chosen; there will be light, joy, and peace, and they will inherit the earth. But for you, the impious, there will be a curse.

5.8 When wisdom is given to the chosen they will all live, and will not again do wrong, either through forgetfulness, or through pride. But those who possess wisdom will be humble.

5.9 They will not again do wrong, and they will not be judged in all the days of their life, and they will not die of wrath or anger. But they will complete the number of the days of their life. And their life will grow in peace, and the years of their joy will increase in gladness and eternal peace; all the days of their life.

6.1 And it came to pass, when the sons of men had increased, that in those days there were born to them fair and beautiful daughters.

6.2 And the Angels, the sons of Heaven, saw them and desired them. And they said to one another: "Come, let us choose for ourselves wives, from the children of men, and let us beget, for ourselves, children."

6.3 And Semyaza, who was their leader, said to them:

"I fear that you may not wish this deed to be done and that I alone will pay for this great sin."

6.4 And they all answered him, and said:

"Let us all swear an oath, and bind one another with curses, so not to alter this plan, but to carry out this plan effectively."

6.5 Then they all swore together and all bound one another with curses to it.

6.6 And they were, in all, two hundred and they came down on Ardis, which is the summit of Mount Hermon. And they called the mountain Hermon because on it they swore and bound one another with curses.

6.7 And these are the names of their leaders:

Semyaza, who was their leader, Ura-kiba (Araqiel), Rameel, Kokabiel, Tamiel, Ramiel, Daniel, Ezeqiel, Baraqiel, Asael, Armaros, Batariel, Ananel, Zaqiel, Samsiel, Satariel, Turiel, Yomiel, Sariel. (see Ch **8** & Ch **69**)

6.8 These are the leaders of the two hundred Angels and of all the others with them.

7.1 And they took wives for themselves, and everyone chose for himself one each. And they began to go into them and were promiscuous with them. And they taught them charms and spells, and they showed them the cutting of roots and trees.

7.2 And they became pregnant and bore large giants. And their height was three thousand cubits.

7.3 These devoured all the toil of men; until men were unable to sustain them.

7.4 And the giants turned against them in order to devour men.

7.5 And they began to sin against birds, and against animals, and against reptiles, and against fish, and they devoured one another's flesh, and drank the blood from it.

7.6 Then the Earth complained about the lawless ones.

8.1 And Azazel taught men to make swords, and daggers, and shields, and breastplates. And he showed them the things after these, and the art of making them; bracelets, and ornaments, and the art of making up the eyes, and of beautifying the eyelids, and the most precious stones, and all kinds of colored dyes. And the world was changed.

8.2 And there was great impiety, and much fornication, and they went astray, and all their ways became corrupt.

8.3 Amezarak taught all those who cast spells and cut roots, Armaros the release of spells, and Baraqiel astrologers, and Kokabiel portents, and Tamiel taught astrology, and Asradel taught the path of the Moon.

8.4 And at the destruction of men they cried out; and their voices reached Heaven.

9.1 And then Michael, Gabriel, Suriel and Uriel, looked down from Heaven and saw the mass of blood that was being shed on the earth and all the iniquity that was being done on the earth.

9.2 And they said to one another: "Let the devastated Earth cry out with the sound of their cries, up to the Gate of Heaven.

9.3 And now to you, Oh Holy Ones of Heaven, the souls of men complain, saying: "Bring our complaint before the Most High."

9.4 And they said to their Lord, the King: "Lord of Lords, God of Gods, King of Kings! Your glorious throne endures for all the generations of the world, and blessed and praised!

9.5 You have made everything, and power over everything is yours. And everything is uncovered, and open, in front of you, and you see everything, and there is nothing that can be hidden from you.

9.6 See then what Azazel has done; how he has taught all iniquity on the earth and revealed the eternal secrets that are made in Heaven.

9.7 And Semyaza has made known spells, he to whom you gave authority to rule over those who are with him.

9.8 And they went into the daughters of men together, lay with those women, became unclean, and revealed to them these sins.

9.9 And the women bore giants, and thereby the whole Earth has been filled with blood and iniquity.

9.10 And now behold the souls which have died cry out and complain unto the Gate of Heaven, and their lament has ascended, and they cannot go out in the face of the iniquity which is being committed on the earth.

9.11 And you know everything, before it happens, and you know this, and what concerns each of them. But you say nothing to us. What ought we to do with them, about this?"

10.1 And then the Most High, the Great and Holy One, spoke and sent Arsyalalyur to the son of Lamech, and said to him:

10.2 "Say to him in my name; hide yourself! And reveal to him the end, which is coming, because the whole earth will be destroyed. A deluge is about to come on all the earth; and all that is in it will be destroyed.

10.3 And now teach him so that he may escape and his offspring may survive for the whole Earth."

10.4 And further the Lord said to Raphael: "Bind Azazel by his hands and his feet and throw him into the darkness. And split open the desert, which is in Dudael, and throw him there.

10.5 And throw on him jagged and sharp stones and cover him with darkness. And let him stay there forever. And cover his face so that he may not see the light.

10.6 And so that, on the Great Day of Judgment, he may be hurled into the fire.

10.7 And restore the Earth which the Angels have ruined. And announce the restoration of the Earth. For I shall restore the Earth so that not all the sons of men shall be destroyed because of the knowledge which the Watchers made known and taught to their sons.

10.8 And the whole Earth has been ruined by the teaching of the works of Azazel; and against him write: ALL SIN."

10.9 And the Lord said to Gabriel: "Proceed against the bastards, and the reprobates, and against the sons of the fornicators. And destroy the sons of the fornicators, and the sons of the Watchers, from amongst men. And send them out, and send them against one another, and let them destroy themselves in battle; for they will not have length of days.

10.10 And they will petition you, but the petitioners will gain nothing in respect of them, for they hope for eternal life, and that each of them will live life for five hundred years."

10.11 And the Lord said to Michael: "Go, inform Semyaza, and the others with him, who have associated with the women to corrupt themselves with them in all their uncleanness.

10.12 When all their sons kill each other, and when they see the destruction of their loved ones, bind them for seventy generations, under the hills of the earth, until the day of their judgment and of their consummation, until the judgment, which is for all eternity, is accomplished.

10.13 And in those days, they will lead them to the Abyss of Fire; in torment, and in prison they will be shut up for all eternity.

10.14 And then Semyaza will be burnt, and from then on destroyed with them; together they will be bound until the end of all generations.

10.15 And destroy all the souls of lust, and the sons of the Watchers, for they have wronged men.

10.16 Destroy all wrong from the face of the Earth and every evil work will cease.

10.17 And now all the righteous will be humble, and will live until they beget thousands. And all the days of their youth, and their sabbaths, they will fulfill in peace.

10.18 And in those days the whole earth will be tilled in righteousness and all of it will be planted with trees; and it will be filled with blessing.

10.19 And all the pleasant trees they will plant on it and they will plant on it vines. And the vine that is planted on it will produce fruit in abundance; and every seed that is sown on it, each measure will produce a thousand, and each measure of olives will produce ten baths of oil.

10.20 And you cleanse the Earth from all wrong, and from all iniquity, and from all sin, and from all impiety, and from all the uncleanness which is brought about on the earth.

10.21 And all the sons of men shall be righteous, and all the nations shall serve and bless me and all shall worship me.

10.22 And the Earth will be cleansed from all corruption, and from all sin, and from all wrath, and from all torment; and I will not again send a flood upon it, for all generations, forever.

11.1 And in those days, I will open the Storehouses of Blessing, which are in Heaven, so that I may send them down upon the Earth, upon the work, and upon the toil, of the sons of men.

11.2 Peace and truth will be united, for all the days of eternity, and for all the generations of eternity.

12.1 And then Enoch disappeared and none of the sons of men knew where he was hidden, where he was, or what had happened.

12.2 And all his doings were with the Holy Ones, and with the Watchers, in his days.

12.3 And I Enoch, was blessing the Great Lord and the King of Eternity. And behold, the Watchers called to me - Enoch the scribe - and said to me:

12.4 "Enoch, scribe of righteousness. Go and inform the Watchers of Heaven, who have left the High Heaven and the Holy Eternal Place, and have corrupted themselves with women, and have done as the sons of men do and have taken wives for themselves and have become completely corrupt on the earth.

12.5 They will have on Earth, neither peace, nor forgiveness of sin, for they will not rejoice in their sons.

12.6 The slaughter of their beloved ones they will see; and over the destruction of their sons they will lament and petition forever. But they will have neither mercy nor peace."

13.1 And Enoch went and said to Azazel: "You will not have peace. A severe sentence has come out against you that you should be bound.

13.2 And you will have neither rest nor mercy, nor the granting of any petitions, because of the wrong which you have taught, and because of all the works of blasphemy and wrong and sin which you have shown to the sons of men."

13.3 And then I went and spoke to them all together, and they were all afraid; fear and trembling seized them.

13.4 And they asked me to write out for them the record of a petition, so that they might receive forgiveness, and to take a record of their petition up to the Lord in Heaven.

13.5 For they were not able, from then on, to speak, and they did not raise their eyes to Heaven, out of shame for the sins, for which they had been condemned.

13.6 And then I wrote out the record of their petition, and their supplication in regard to their spirits, and the deeds of each one of them, and in regard to what they asked; that they should obtain absolution and forbearance.

13.7 And I went and sat down by the waters of Dan, in Dan, which is southwest of Hermon; and I read out the record of their petition, until I fell asleep.

13.8 And behold a dream came to me, and visions fell upon me, and I saw a vision of wrath; that I should speak to the sons of Heaven and reprove them.

13.9 And I woke up and went to them, and they were all sitting gathered as they mourned, in Ubelseyael, which is between Lebanon and Senir, with their faces covered.

13.10 And I spoke in front of them all; the visions that I had seen in my sleep, and I began to speak these words to reprove the Watchers of Heaven.

14.1 This book is the word of righteousness, and of reproof, for the Watchers who are from Eternity; as the Holy and Great One commanded in that vision.

14.2 I saw in my sleep what I will now tell, with the tongue of flesh, and with my breath, which the Great One has given men in the mouth, so that they might speak with it, and understand with the heart.

14.3 As He has created, and appointed, men to understand the word of knowledge, so He created and appointed me to reprove the Watchers, the sons of Heaven.

14.4 And I wrote out your petition, but in my vision, thus it appeared, that your petition would not be granted to you, for all the days of eternity; and complete judgment has been decreed against you, and you will not have peace.

14.5 And from now on, you will not ascend into Heaven, for all eternity, and it has been decreed that you will be bound on Earth for all the days of eternity.

14.6 And before this, you will have seen the destruction of your beloved sons, and you will not be able to enjoy them, but they will fall before you by the sword.

14.7 And your petition will not be granted in respect of them or in respect of yourselves. And while you weep and supplicate you do not speak a single word from the writings which I have written.

14.8 And the vision appeared to me, as follows: - Behold; clouds called me in the vision, and mist called me. And the path of the stars, and flashes of lightning, hastened me and drove me. And in the vision winds caused me to fly, and hastened me, and lifted me up into the sky.

14.9 And I proceeded until I came near a wall which was made of hailstones, and a tongue of fire surrounded it, and it began to make me afraid.

14.10 And I went into the tongue of fire and came near to a large house, which was built of hailstones, and the wall of that house was like a mosaic of hailstones and its floor was snow.

14.11 Its roof was like the path of the stars and flashes of lightning, and among them was fiery cherubim, and their sky was like water.

14.12 And there was a fire burning around its wall and its door was ablaze with fire.

14.13 And I went into that house, and it was as hot as fire and as cold as snow, and there was neither pleasure nor life in it. Fear covered me and trembling took hold of me.

14.14 And as I was shaking and trembling, I fell on my face.

14.15 And I saw in the vision, and behold, another house which was larger than the former and all its doors were open before me, and it was built of a tongue of fire.

14.16 And in everything, it so excelled in glory and splendor and size, so that I am unable to describe to you its glory and its size.

14.17 And its floor was fire, and above lightning and the path of the stars, and its roof also was a burning fire.

14.18 And I looked, and I saw in it, a high throne, and its appearance was like ice, and its surrounds like the shining Sun and the sound of cherubim.

14.19 And from underneath the high throne there flowed out rivers of fire so that it was impossible to look at it.

14.20 And He who is Great in Glory sat upon it, and his raiment was brighter than the Sun, and whiter than any snow.

14.21 And no Angel could enter, and at the appearance of the face of Him who is Honoured and Praised, no creature of flesh could look.

14.22 A sea of fire burnt around Him, and a great fire stood in front of Him, and none of those around Him came near to Him. Ten thousand times ten thousand stood before Him but He needed no Holy Council.

14.23 And the Holy Ones who were near to Him did not leave by night or day and did not depart from Him.

14.24 And until then I had a covering on my face, as I trembled. And the Lord called me with his own mouth, and said to me: "Come here, Enoch, to my Holy Word."

14.25 And He lifted me up and brought me near to the door. And I looked, with my face down.

15.1 And He answered me, and said to me with His voice: "Hear! Do not be afraid, Enoch, you righteous man, and scribe of righteousness. Come here and hear my voice.

15.2 And go say to the Watchers of Heaven, who sent you to petition on their behalf: You ought to petition on behalf of men, not men on behalf of you.

15.3 Why have you left the High, Holy and Eternal Heaven, and lain with women, and become unclean with the daughters of men, and taken wives for yourselves, and done as the sons of the earth, and begotten giant sons?

15.4 And you were spiritual, Holy, living an eternal life, but you became unclean upon the women, and begot children through the blood of flesh, and lusted after the blood of men, and produced flesh and blood, as they do, who die and are destroyed.

15.5 And for this reason I give men wives; so that they might sow seed in them, and so that children might be born by them, so that deeds might be done on the Earth.

15.6 But you, formerly, were spiritual, living an eternal, immortal life, for all the generations of the world.

15.7 For this reason I did not arrange wives for you; because the dwelling of the spiritual ones is in Heaven.

15.8 And now, the giants who were born from body and flesh will be called Evil Spirits on the Earth, and on the Earth will be their dwelling.

15.9 And evil spirits came out from their flesh, because from above they were created, from the Holy Watchers was their origin and first foundation. Evil spirits they will be on Earth and 'Spirits of the Evil Ones' they will be called.

15.10 And the dwelling of the Spirits of Heaven is Heaven, but the dwelling of the spirits of the Earth, who were born on the Earth, is Earth.

15.11 And the spirits of the giants do wrong, are corrupt, attack, fight, break on the Earth, and cause sorrow. And they eat no food, do not thirst, and are not observed.

15.12 And these spirits will rise against the sons of men, and against the women, because they came out of them during the days of slaughter and destruction.

16.1 And the death of the giants, wherever the spirits have gone out from their bodies, their flesh will be destroyed, before the Judgment. Thus they will be destroyed until the Day of the Great Consummation is accomplished, upon the Great Age, upon the Watchers and the impious ones."

16.2 And now to the Watchers, who sent you to petition on their behalf, who were formerly in Heaven:

16.3 "You were in Heaven but its secrets had not yet been revealed to you; and a worthless mystery you knew. This you made known to women, in the hardness of your hearts. And through this mystery the women and the men cause evil to increase on the Earth." **16.4** Say to them therefore: "You will not have peace."

17.1 And they took me to a place where they were like burning fire, and, when they wished, they made themselves look like men.

17.2 And they led me to a place of storm, and to a mountain, the tip of whose summit reached to Heaven.

17.3 And I saw lighted places, and thunder in the outermost ends, in its depths a bow of fire, and arrows and their quivers, and a sword of fire, and all the flashes of lightning.

17.4 And they took me to the Water of Life, as it is called, and to the Fire of the West, which receives every setting of the Sun.

17.5 And I came to a river of fire, whose fire flows like water, and pours out into the Great Sea, which is towards the west.

17.6 And I saw all the great rivers, and I reached the Great Darkness, and went where all flesh walks.

17.7 And I saw the Mountains of the Darkness of Winter and the place where the water of all the deeps pours out.

17.8 And I saw the mouths of all the rivers of the Earth, and the mouth of the deep.

18.1 And I saw the storehouses of all the winds, and I saw how with them He has adorned all creation, and I saw the foundations of the Earth.

18.2 And I saw the cornerstone of the Earth. And I saw the four winds which support the Earth and the sky.

18.3 And I saw how the winds stretch out the height of Heaven, and how they position themselves between Heaven and Earth; they are the Pillars of Heaven.

18.4 And I saw the winds which turn the sky and cause the disc of the Sun and all the stars to set.

18.5 And I saw the winds on the Earth which support the clouds and I saw the paths of the Angels. I saw at the end of the Earth; the firmament of Heaven above.

18.6 And I went towards the south, and it was burning day and night, where there were seven mountains of precious stones, three towards the east and three towards the south.

18.7 And those towards the east were of coloured stone, and one was of pearl, and one of healing stone; and those towards the south, of red stone.

18.8 And the middle one reached to Heaven, like the throne of the Lord, of stibium, and the top of the throne was of sapphire.

18.9 And I saw a burning fire, and what was in all the mountains.

18.10 And I saw a place there, beyond the great earth; there the waters gathered together.

18.11 And I saw a deep chasm of the earth, with pillars of heavenly fire, and I saw among them fiery pillars of Heaven, which were falling, and as regards both height and depth, they were immeasurable.

18.12 And beyond this chasm, I saw a place, and it had neither the sky above it, nor the foundation of earth below it; there was no water on it, and no birds, but it was a desert place.

18.13 And a terrible thing I saw there, seven stars, like great burning mountains.

18.14 And like a spirit questioning me, the Angel said: "This is the place of the end of Heaven and Earth; this is the prison for the Stars of Heaven and the Host of Heaven.

18.15 And the stars which roll over the fire, these are the ones which transgressed the command of the Lord, from the beginning of their rising, because they did not come out at their proper times.

18.16 And He was angry with them, and bound them until the time of the consummation of their sin, in the Year of Mystery."

19.1 And Uriel said to me: "The spirits of the Angels who were promiscuous with women will stand here; and they, assuming many forms, made men unclean and will lead men astray so that they sacrifice to demons as gods. And they will stand there until the great judgment day, on which they will be judged, so that an end will be made of them.

19.2 And their wives, having led astray the Angels of Heaven, will become peaceful."

19.3 And I, Enoch, alone saw the sight, the ends of everything; and no man has seen what I have seen.

20.1 And these are the names of the Holy Angels who keep watch.

20.2 Uriel, one of the Holy Angels; namely the Holy Angel of the Spirits of Men.

20.4 Raguel, one of the Holy Angels; who takes vengeance on the world, and on the lights.

20.5 Michael, one of the Holy Angels, namely the one put in charge of the best part of humankind, in charge of the nation.

20.6 Saraqael, one of the Holy Angels; who is in charge of the spirits of men who cause the spirits to sin.

20.7 Gabriel, one of the Holy Angels, who is in charge of the Serpents, and the Garden, and the Cherubim.

21.1 And I went round to a place where nothing was made.

21.2 And I saw a terrible thing, neither the High Heaven nor the firm ground, but a desert place, prepared and terrible.

21.3 And there, I saw seven Stars of Heaven, bound on it together, like great mountains, and burning like fire.

21.4 Then I said: "For what sin have they been bound, and why have they been thrown here?"

21.5 And Uriel, one of the Holy Angels, who was with me and led me, spoke to me and said: "Enoch, about whom do you ask? About whom do you inquire, ask, and care?

21.6 These are some of the stars which transgressed the command of the Lord Most High, and they have been bound here until ten thousand ages are completed; the number of days of their sin."

21.7 And from there I went to another place, more terrible than this. And I saw a terrible thing: there was a great fire there, which burnt and blazed. And the place had a cleft reaching into the abyss, full of great pillars of fire, which were made to fall; neither its extent nor its size could I see, nor could I see its source.

21.8 Then I said: "How terrible this place is, and how painful to look at!"

21.9 Then Uriel, one of the Holy Angels, who was with me, answered me. He answered me and said to me: "Enoch, why do you have such fear and terror because of this terrible place, and before this pain?"

21.10 And he said to me: "This place is the prison of the Angels, and there they will be held for ever."

22.1 And from there, I went to another place, and he showed me in the west a large and high mountain, and a hard rock, and four beautiful places.

22.2 And inside, it was deep, wide, and very smooth. How smooth is that which rolls, and deep and dark to look at!

22.3 Then Raphael, one of the Holy Angels who was with me, answered me, and said to me: "These beautiful places are there so that the spirits, the souls of the dead, might be gathered into them. For them they were created; so that here they might gather the souls of the sons of men.

22.4 And these places they made, where they will keep them until the Day of Judgment, and until their appointed time, and that appointed time will be long, until the great judgment comes upon them.

22.5 And I saw the spirits of the sons of men who were dead and their voices reached Heaven and complained.

22.6 Then I asked Raphael, the Angel who was with me, and said to him: "Whose is this spirit, whose voice thus reaches Heaven and complains?"

22.7 And he answered me, and said to me, saying: "This spirit is the one that came out of Abel, whom Cain, his brother, killed. And he will complain about him until his offspring are destroyed from the face of the Earth, and from amongst the offspring of men, his offspring perish."

22.8 Then I asked about him, and about judgment on all, and I said: "Why is one separated from another?"

22.9 And he answered me, and said to me: "These three places where made, in order that they might separate the spirits of the dead. And thus the souls of the righteous have been separated; this is the spring of water, and on it the light.

22.10 Likewise, a place has been created for sinners, when they die, and are buried in the earth, and judgment has not come upon them during their life.

22.11 And here their souls will be separated for this great torment, until the Great Day of Judgment and Punishment and Torment for those who curse, forever, and of vengeance on their souls. And there he will bind them forever. Verily, He is, from the beginning of the world.

22.12 And thus a place has been separated for the souls of those who complain, and give information about their destruction, about when they were killed, in the days of the sinners.

22.13 Thus a place has been created, for the souls of men who are not righteous, but sinners, accomplished in wrongdoing, and with the wrongdoers will be their lot. But their souls will not be killed on the day of judgment, nor will they rise from here."

22.14 Then I blessed the Lord of Glory, and said: "Blessed be my Lord, the Lord of Glory and Righteousness, who rules everything forever."

23.1 And from there I went to another place, towards the west, to the ends of the Earth.

23.2 And I saw a fire that burnt and ran, without resting or ceasing from running, by day or by night, but continued in exactly the same way.

23.3 And I asked saying: "What is this which has no rest?"

23.4 Then Raguel, one of the Holy Angels, who was with me, answered me, and said to me: "This burning fire, whose course you saw towards the west,

is the fire of all the Lights of Heaven."

24.1 And from there I went to another place of the Earth and he showed me a mountain of fire that blazed day and night.

24.2 And I went towards it and saw seven magnificent mountains. And all were different from one another, and precious and beautiful stones, and all were precious, and their appearance glorious, and their form was beautiful. Three towards the east one fixed firmly on another and three towards the south one on another, and deep and rugged valleys, no one of which was near another.

24.3 And there was a seventh mountain, in the middle of these, and in their height they were all like the seat of a throne and fragrant trees surrounded it.

24.4 And there was among them a tree such as which I have never smelt, and none of them, or any others, were like it. It smells more fragrant than any fragrance, and its leaves, and its flowers, and its wood never wither. Its fruit is good, and its fruit is like bunches of dates on a palm.

24.5 And then I said: "Behold, this beautiful tree! Beautiful to look at, and

pleasant are its leaves, and its fruit very delightful in appearance."

24.6 And then Michael, one of the Holy and Honoured Angels, who was with me, and was in charge of them,

25.1 answered me and said to me: "Enoch, why do you ask me about the fragrance of this tree, and why do you inquire to learn?"

25.2 Then I, Enoch, answered him saying: "I wish to learn about everything, but especially about this tree."

25.3 And he answered me, saying: "This high mountain, which you saw, whose summit is like the Throne of the Lord, is the throne where the Holy and Great One, the Lord of Glory, the Eternal King, will sit, when he comes down to visit the Earth for good.

25.4 And this beautiful and fragrant tree, and no creature of flesh has authority to touch it until the great judgment, when he will take vengeance on all and bring everything to a consummation forever, this will be given to the righteous and the humble.

25.5 From its fruit, life will be given to the chosen; towards the north it will be planted, in a Holy place, by the house of the Lord, the Eternal King.

25.6 Then they will rejoice with joy and be glad in the Holy place. They will each draw the fragrance of it into their bones, and they will live a long life on earth, as your fathers lived. And in their days sorrow and pain, and toil and punishment, will not touch them."

25.7 Then I blessed the Lord of Glory, the Eternal King, because he has prepared such things for righteous men, and has created such things, and said that they are to be given to them.

26.1 And from there, I went to the middle of the earth, and saw a blessed, well watered place, which had branches which remained alive, and sprouted from a tree which had been cut down.

26.2 And there I saw a holy mountain, and under the mountain, to the east of it, there was water, and it flowed towards the south.

26.3 And I saw towards the east, another mountain, which was of the same height, and between them, there was a deep and narrow valley; and in it, a stream ran by the mountain.

26.4 And to the west of this one, was another mountain, which was lower than it was and not high; and under it, there was a valley between them. And there were other deep and dry valleys at the end of the three mountains.

26.5 And all the valleys were deep and narrow, of hard rock, and trees were planted on them.

26.6 And I was amazed at the rock, and I was amazed at the valley; I was very much amazed.

27.1 Then I said: "What is the purpose of this blessed land, which is completely full of trees, and of this accursed valley in the middle of them?"

27.2 Then Raphael, one of the Holy Angels who was with me, answered me, and said to me: "This accursed valley, is for those who are cursed for ever. Here will be gathered together all who speak with their mouths against the Lord - words that are not fitting, and say hard things about His Glory. Here they will gather them together, and here will be their place of judgment.

27.3 And in the last days there will be the spectacle of the righteous judgment upon them, in front of the righteous, forever. For here, the merciful will bless the Lord of Glory the Eternal King.

27.4 And in the days of the judgment on them they will bless Him, on account of his mercy, according as He has assigned to them their lot."

27.5 Then I myself blessed the Lord of Glory, I addressed Him, and I remembered His majesty, as was fitting.

28.1 And from there, I went towards the east, to the middle of the mountain of the wilderness, and I saw only desert.

28.2 But it was full of trees from this seed and water gushed out over it from above.

28.3 The torrent, which flowed towards the northwest, seemed copious, and from all sides, there went up spray and mist.

29.1 And I went to another place, away from the wilderness; I came near to the east of this mountain.

29.2 And there I saw Trees of Judgment, especially vessels of the fragrance of incense and myrrh, and the trees were not alike.

30.1 And above it, above these, above the mountains of the east, and not far away, I saw another place, valleys of water, like that which does not fail.

30.2 And I saw a beautiful tree, and its fragrance was like that of the mastic.

30.3 And by the banks of these valleys I saw fragrant cinnamon. And beyond those valleys I came towards the east.

31

31.1 And I saw another mountain on which there were trees, and there flowed out water, and there flowed out from it, as it were, a nectar whose name is styrax and galbanum.

31.2 And beyond this mountain I saw another mountain, and on it there were aloe trees, and those trees were full of a fruit, which is like an almond, and is hard.

31.3 And when they take this fruit it is better than any fragrance.

32

32.1 And after these fragrances, to the north, as I looked over the mountains, I saw seven mountains full of fine nard, and fragrant trees of cinnamon and pepper.

32.2 And from there, I went over the summits of those mountains, far away to the east, and I went over the Red Sea, and I was far from it, and I went over the Angel Zotiel.

32.3 And I came to the Garden of Righteousness, and I saw beyond those trees many large trees growing there, sweet smelling, large, very beautiful and glorious, the Trees of Wisdom, from which they eat and know great wisdom.

32.4 And it is like the carob tree, and its fruit is like bunches of grapes on a vine, very beautiful, and the smell of this tree spreads and penetrates afar.

32.5 And I said: "This tree is beautiful! How beautiful and pleasing is its appearance!"

32.6 And the Holy Angel Raphael, who was with me, answered me and said to me: "This is the Tree of Wisdom, from which your ancient father and ancient mother, who were before you, ate and learnt wisdom; and their eyes were opened, and they knew that they were naked. And they were driven from the garden."

33

33.1 And from there I went to the ends of the earth, and I saw there large animals, each different from the other, and also birds, which differed in form, beauty, and call - each different from the other.

33.2 And to the east of these animals, I saw the ends of the Earth, on which Heaven rests, and the open Gates of Heaven.

33.3 And I saw how the stars of Heaven come out, and counted the Gates out of which they come, and wrote down all their outlets, for each one, individually, according to their number. And their names, according to their constellations, their positions, their times, and their months, as the Angel Uriel, who was with me, showed me.

33.4 And he showed me everything, and wrote it down, and also their names he wrote down for me, and their laws and their functions.

34

34.1 And from there I went towards the north, to the ends of the Earth, and there I saw a great and glorious wonder at the ends of the whole Earth.

34.2 And there I saw three Gates of Heaven; through each of them north winds go out; when they blow there is cold, hail, hoarfrost, snow, fog, and rain.

34.3 And from one Gate, it blows for good; but when they blow through the other two Gates, it is with force, and it brings torment over the earth, and they blow with force.

35.1 And from there I went towards the west, to the ends of the Earth, and I saw there, as I saw in the east, three open Gates - as many Gates and as many outlets.

36.1 And from there I went towards the south, to the ends of the Earth, and there I saw three Gates of Heaven open; and the south wind, the mist, and the rain, and wind, come out from there.

36.2 And from there I went towards the east of the ends of Heaven, and there I saw the three eastern Gates of Heaven open, and above them, there were smaller Gates.

36.3 Through each of these smaller Gates, the stars of Heaven pass, and go towards the west, on the path that has been shown to them.

36.4 And when I saw, I blessed, and I will always bless the Lord of Glory, who has made Great and Glorious Wonders so that he might show the greatness of His Work, to His Angels, and to the souls of men, so that they might praise His Work. And so that all his creatures might see the work of His Power, and praise the great work of His Hands, and bless Him forever!

SECTION II.
CHAPTERS XXXVII
THE PARABLES

37.1 The second vision that he saw, the vision of wisdom, which Enoch, the son of Jared, the son of Malalel, the son of Cainan, the son of Enosh, the son of Seth, the son of Adam, saw.
37.2 And this is the beginning of the words of wisdom, which I raised my voice to speak, and say. "To those who dwell on dry ground: - Hear, you men of old, and see, those who come after; the words of the Holy One, which I will speak, in front of the Lord of Spirits."

37.3 "It would have been better to have said these things before, but from those who come after, we will not withhold the beginning of wisdom."

37.4 Until now, there has not been given, by the Lord of Spirits, such wisdom as I have received. In accordance with my insight, in accordance with the wish of the Lord of Spirits: by whom the lot of eternal life has been given to me.

37.5 And the three parables were imparted to me and I raised my voice, and said to those who dwell on the dry ground: -

38.1 The First Parable.
When the community of the righteous appears and the sinners are judged for their sins and are driven from the face of the dry ground.

38.2 And when the Righteous One appears, in front of the chosen righteous, whose works are weighed by the Lord of Spirits. And when light appears to the righteous and chosen who dwell on the dry ground. Where will be the dwelling of the sinners? And where will be the resting-place of those who denied the Lord of Spirits? It would have been better for them, if they had not been born.

38.3 And when the secrets of the righteous are revealed, the sinners will be judged, and the impious driven from the presence of the righteous and the chosen.

38.4 And from then on, those who possess the earth will not be mighty and exalted. Nor will they be able to look at the face of the Holy ones, for the light of the Lord of the Spirits will have appeared on the face of the Holy, the righteous, and the chosen.

38.5 And the mighty kings will at that time be destroyed and given into the hand of the righteous and the Holy.

38.6 And from then on no one will be able to seek the Lord of Spirits for their life will be at an end.

39.1 And it will come to pass in these days that the chosen and holy children will come down from the high Heavens and their offspring will become one with the sons of men. 39.2 In those days Enoch received books of indignation and anger and books of tumult and confusion. And there will be no mercy for them, says the Lord of Spirits.

39.3 And at that time clouds and a storm wind carried me off from the face of the earth and set me down at the end of Heaven.

39.4 And there I saw another vision; the Dwelling of the Righteous and the Resting-Places of the Holy.

39.5 There my eyes saw their dwelling with the Angels, and their resting places with the Holy Ones, and they were petitioning and supplicating and praying, on behalf of the sons of men; and righteousness, like water, flowed in front of them, and mercy like dew on the ground. Thus it is among them forever and ever.

39.6 And in those days my eyes saw the Place of the Chosen Ones of Righteousness and Faith; and there will be righteousness in their days, and the righteous and chosen will be without number, in front of him, forever and ever.

39.7 And I saw their dwelling, under the Wings of the Lord of Spirits, and all the righteous and chosen shone in front of him, like the light of fire. And their mouths were full of blessing, and their lips praised the name of the Lord of Spirits. And righteousness will not fail in front of him, and truth will not fail in front of him.

39.8 There I wished to dwell, and my soul longed for that dwelling; there had my lot been assigned before, for thus it was decided about me, in front of the Lord of Spirits.

39.9 And in those days I praised and exalted the name of the Lord of Spirits, with blessing and praise, for he has destined me for blessing and praise, in accordance with the Lord of Spirits.

39.10 And for a long time my eyes looked at that place, and I blessed him and praised him, saying: "Blessed is He, and may He be blessed from the beginning and for ever!"

39.11 And in his presence there is no end. He knew before the world was created what the world would be, even for all the generations that are to come.

39.12 Those who do not sleep bless you, and they stand before Your Glory, and bless and praise and exalt, saying: "Holy, Holy, Holy, Lord of Spirits; he fills the earth with spirits."

39.13 And there, my eyes saw all those who do not sleep; standing in front of Him, and blessing, and saying: "Blessed are you, and blessed is the name of the Lord, for ever and ever!"

39.14 And my face was transformed until I was unable to see.

40.1 And after this I saw a thousand thousands and ten thousand times ten thousand! A multitude beyond number, or reckoning, who stood in front of the Glory of the Lord of Spirits.

40.2 I looked, and on the four sides of the Lord of Spirits, I saw four figures, different from those who were standing; and I learnt their names, because the Angel who went with me made known their names, and showed me all the secret things.

40.3 And I heard the voices of those four figures as they sang praises in front of the Lord of Glory.

40.4 The first voice blesses the Lord of Spirits forever and ever.

40.5 And the second voice I heard blessing the Chosen One and the chosen who depend on the Lord of Spirits.

40.6 And the third voice I heard, petitioned, and prayed, on behalf of those who dwell on dry ground and supplicate in the name of the Lord of Spirits.

40.7 And the fourth voice I heard driving away the Satans and not allowing them to come in front of the Lord of Spirits to accuse those who dwell on the high ground. **40.8** And after this I asked the Angel of Peace, who went with me, and showed me everything which is secret: "Who are those four figures, whom I have seen, and whose words I have heard and written down?"

40.9 And he said to me: "This first one, is the Holy Michael, the merciful and long-suffering. And the second, who is in charge of all the diseases, and in charge of all the wounds of the sons of men, is Raphael. And the third, who is in charge of all the powers, is the Holy Gabriel. And the fourth, who is in charge of repentance and hope of those who will inherit eternal life, is Phanuel."

40.10 And these are the four Angels of the Lord Most High; and the four voices that I heard in those days.

41.1 And after this, I saw all the secrets of Heaven, and how the Kingdom is divided, and how the deeds of men are weighed in the Balance.

41.2 There I saw the Dwelling of the Chosen, and the Resting Places of the Holy; and my eyes saw there all the sinners who deny the name of the Lord of Spirits being driven from there. And they dragged them off, and they were not able to remain, because of the punishment that went out from the Lord of Spirits.

41.3 And there my eyes saw the secrets of the flashes of lightning and of the thunder. And the secrets of the winds, how they are distributed in order to blow over the earth, and the

THE BOOKS OF ENOCH

secrets of the clouds, and of the dew; and there I saw from where they go out, in that place. And how, from there, the dust of the earth is saturated. **41.4** And there I saw closed store-houses from which the winds are distributed, and the storehouse of the hail, and the storehouse of the mist, and the storehouse of the clouds; and its cloud remained over the earth, from the beginning of the world.

41.5 And I saw the Chambers of the Sun and the Moon, where they go out, and where they return. And their glorious return; and how one is more honoured than the other is. And their magnificent course, and how they do not leave their course, neither adding nor subtracting from their course. And how they keep faith in one another, observing their oath.

41.6 And the Sun goes out first, and completes its journey at the command of the Lord of Spirits - and his Name endures forever and ever.

41.7 And after this is the hidden, and visible, path of the Moon, and it travels the course of its journey, in that place, by day and by night. One stands opposite the other, in front of the Lord of Spirits, and they give thanks, and sing praise, and do not rest, because their thanksgiving is like rest to them.

41.8 For the shining Sun makes many revolutions; for a blessing and for a curse. And the path of the journey of the Moon is for the righteous light but for the sinners; darkness. In the Name of the Lord, who has created a division between light and darkness, and has divided the spirits of men, and has established the spirits of the righteous, in the name of His Righteousness.

41.9 For no Angel hinders, and no power is able to hinder, because the judge sees them all, and judges them all Himself.

42.1 Wisdom found no place where she could dwell, and her dwelling was in Heaven.

42.2 Wisdom went out, in order to dwell among the sons of men, but did not find a dwelling; wisdom returned to her place, and took her seat in the midst of the Angels.

42.3 And iniquity came out from her chambers; those whom she did not seek she found, and dwelt among them, like rain in the desert, and like dew on the parched ground.

43.1 And again I saw flashes of lightning and the stars of Heaven, and I saw how He called them all by their names, and they obeyed Him.

43.2 And I saw the Balance of Righteousness, how they are weighed according to their light, according to the width of their areas, and the day of their appearing. And how their revolutions produce lightning, and I saw their revolutions, according to the number of the Angels, and how they keep faith with one another.

43.3 And I asked the Angel, who went with me and showed me what is secret: "What are these?"

43.4 And he said to me: "Their likeness, the Lord of Spirits has shown to you; these are the names of the righteous who, dwell on the dry ground and believe in the name of the Lord of Spirits for ever and ever."

44.1 And other things I saw concerning lightning, how some of the stars rise and become lightning but cannot lose their form.

45.1 **The Second Parable**.
About those who deny the Name of the Dwelling of the Holy Ones and of the Lord of Spirits.

45.2 They will not ascend into Heaven nor will they come upon the earth; such will be the lot of the sinners who deny the Name of the Lord of Spirits who will thus be kept for the Day of Affliction and Distress.

45.3 "On that day the Chosen One will sit on the Throne of Glory and will choose their works. And their resting places will be without number and their spirits within them will grow strong when they see My Chosen One and those who appeal to My Holy and Glorious Name.

45.4 And on that day I will cause My Chosen One to dwell among them and I will transform Heaven and make it an Eternal Blessing and Light.

45.5 And I will transform the dry ground and make it a blessing, and I will cause My Chosen Ones to dwell upon it; but those who commit sin and evil will not tread upon it.

45.6 For I have seen, and have satisfied with peace, My Righteous Ones, and have placed them in front of Me; but for the sinners My Judgement draws near so that I may destroy them from the face of the earth."

46.1 And there I saw one who had a 'Head of Days' and his head was white like wool. And with him there was another whose face had the appearance of a man and his face was full of grace like one of the Holy Angels.

46.2 And I asked one of the Holy Angels, who went with me and showed me all the secrets, about that Son of Man, who he was, and from where he was, and why he went with the Head of Days.

46.3 And he answered me, and said to me:
"This is the Son of Man who has righteousness and with whom righteousness dwells. He will reveal all the treasures of that which is secret, for the Lord of Spirits has chosen him, and through uprightness his lot has surpassed all others, in front of the Lord of Spirits, forever.

46.4 And this Son of Man, who you have seen, will rouse the kings and the powerful from their resting places, and the strong from their thrones, and will loose the reins of the strong, and will break the teeth of the sinners.

46.5 And he will cast down the kings from their thrones, and from their kingdoms, for they do not exalt him, and do not praise him, and do not humbly acknowledge from where their kingdom was given to them.

46.6 And he will cast down the faces of the strong and shame will fill them, and darkness will be their dwelling, and worms will be their resting place. And they will have no hope of rising from their resting-places, for they do not exalt the name of the Lord of Spirits.

46.7 And these are they who judge the Stars of Heaven, and raise their hands against the Most High, and trample upon the dry ground, and dwell upon it. And all their deeds show iniquity, and their power rests on their riches, and their faith is in their gods that they have made with their hands, and they deny the name of the Lord of Spirits.

46.8 And they will be driven from the houses of his congregation, and of the faithful, who depend on the Name of the Lord of Spirits.

47.1 And in those days, the prayer of the righteous, and the blood of the righteous will have ascended from the Earth in front of the Lord of Spirits.

47.2 In these days the Holy Ones who live in Heaven above will unite with one voice, and supplicate, and pray, and praise, and give thanks, and bless, in the name of the Lord of Spirits. Because of the blood of the righteous that has been poured out. And because of the prayer of the righteous, so that it may not cease in front of the Lord of Spirits, so that justice might be done to them, and that their patience may not have to last forever."

47.3 And in those days, I saw the Head of Days sit down on the Throne of his Glory and the Books of the Living were opened in front of him and all His Host, which dwell in the Heavens above, and his Council were standing in front of Him.

47.4 And the hearts of the Holy Ones were full of joy that the number of righteousness had been reached, and the prayer of the righteous had been heard, and the blood of the righteous had not been required in front of the Lord of Spirits.

48.1 And in that place I saw an inexhaustible spring of righteousness and many springs of wisdom surrounded it, and all the thirsty drank from them and were filled with wisdom, and their dwelling was with the Righteous and the Holy and the Chosen.

48.2 And at that hour that Son of Man was named, in the presence of the Lord of Spirits, and his name brought to the Head of Days.

48.3 Even before the Sun and the constellations were created, before the Stars of Heaven were made, his name was named in front of the Lord of Spirits.

48.4 He will be a staff to the righteous and the Holy, so that they may lean on him and not fall, and he will be the Light of the Nations, and he will be the hope of those who grieve in their hearts.

48.5 All those who dwell upon the dry ground will fall down and worship in front of him, and they will bless, and praise, and celebrate with psalms, the name of the Lord of Spirits.

48.6 And because of this he was chosen, and hidden in front of Him, before the World was created, and forever.

48.7 But the wisdom of the Lord of Spirits has revealed him to the Holy and the righteous, for he has kept safe the lot of the righteous, for they have hated and rejected this world of iniquity. And all its works and its ways they have hated in the name of the Lord of Spirits. For in His name they are saved and he is the one who will require their lives.

48.8 And in those days the kings of the Earth, and the strong who possess the dry ground, will have downcast faces because of the works of their hands, for on the day of their distress and trouble they will not save themselves.

48.9 And I will give them into the hands of my chosen ones; like straw in the fire, and like lead in water, so they will burn in front of the righteous, and sink in front of the Holy, and no trace will be found of them.

48.10 And on the day of their trouble there will be rest on the earth and they will fall down in front of him and will not rise. And there will be no one who will take them with his hands and raise them for they denied the Lord of Spirits and his Messiah. May the name of the Lord of Spirits be blessed!

49.1 For wisdom has been poured out like water and glory will not fail in front of Him forever and ever.

49.2 For He is powerful in all the secrets of righteousness and iniquity will pass away like a shadow, and will have no existence; for the Chosen One stands in front of the Lord of Spirits and His Glory is for ever and ever, and His Power for all generations.

49.3 And in Him dwell the spirit of wisdom, and the spirit that gives understanding, and the spirit of knowledge and of power, and the spirit of those who sleep in righteousness.

49.4 And he will judge the things that are secret, and no one will be able to say an idle word in front of him, for he has been chosen in front of the Lord of Spirits, in accordance with His wish.

50.1 And in those days a change will occur for the Holy and the chosen; the Light of Days will rest upon them, and glory and honour will return to the Holy.

50.2 And on the day of trouble, calamity will be heaped up over the sinners, but the righteous will conquer in the Name of the Lord of Spirits and He will show this to others so that they might repent and abandon the works of their hands.

50.3 And they will have no honour in front of the Lord of Spirits, but in His Name they will be saved and the Lord of Spirits will have mercy on them, for his mercy is great.

50.4 And He is righteous in His judgment, and in front of His Glory iniquity will not be able to stand against His Judgment; he who does not repent will be destroyed.

50.5 "And from then on I will not have mercy on them," says the Lord of Spirits.

51.1 And in those days the Earth will return that which has been entrusted to it, and Sheol will return that which has been entrusted to it and that which it has received. And destruction will return what it owes.

51.2 And He will choose the Righteous and the Holy from among them; for the day has come near when they must be saved.

51.3 And in those days, the Chosen One will sit on his throne, and all the Secrets of Wisdom will flow out from the council of his mouth, for the Lord of Spirits has appointed him and glorified him.

51.4 And in those days the mountains will leap like rams, and the hills will skip like lambs satisfied with milk, and all will become Angels in Heaven. **51.5** Their faces will shine with joy, for in those days the Chosen One will have risen and the earth will rejoice. And the righteous will dwell upon it and the chosen will walk upon it.

52.1 And after those days, in that place where I had seen all the visions of that which is secret, for I had been carried off by a whirlwind, and they had brought me to the west.

52.2 There my eyes saw the secrets of Heaven; everything that will occur on Earth: a mountain of iron, and a mountain of copper, and a mountain of silver, and a mountain of gold, and a mountain of soft metal, and a mountain of lead.

52.3 And I asked the Angel who went with me, saying:

"What are these things which I have seen in secret?"

52.4 And he said to me: "All these things which you have seen serve the authority of His Messiah, so that he may be strong and powerful on the Earth."

52.5 And that Angel of Peace answered me, saying: "Wait a little and you will see, and everything which is secret, which the Lord of Spirits has established, will be revealed to you.

52.6 And these mountains, that you have seen; the mountain of iron, and the mountain of copper, and the mountain of silver, and the mountain of gold, and the mountain of soft metal, and the mountain of lead. All these in front of the Chosen One will be like wax before fire, and like the water that comes down from above onto these mountains they will be weak under his feet.

52.7 And it will come to pass in those days, that neither by gold, nor by silver, will men save themselves; they will be unable to save themselves, or to flee.

52.8 And there will be neither iron for war nor material for a breastplate; bronze will be no use, and tin will be of no use and will count for nothing, and lead will not be wanted.

52.9 All these will be wiped out and destroyed from the face of the earth when the Chosen One appears in front of the Lord of Spirits."

53.1 And there my eyes saw a deep valley, and its mouth was open; and all those who dwell upon dry ground and the sea and the islands will bring gifts and presents and offerings to him, but that deep valley will not become full.

53.2 And their hands commit evil, and everything at which the righteous toil the sinners evilly devour; and so the sinners will be destroyed from in front of the Lord of Spirits, and will be banished from the face of His Earth, unceasingly for ever and ever.

53.3 For I saw the Angels of Punishment going and preparing all the instruments of Satan.

53.4 And I asked the Angel of Peace, who went with me, and I said to him: "These instruments - for whom are they preparing them?"

53.5 And he said to me: "They are preparing these for the kings and the powerful of this Earth, so that by means of them they may be destroyed.

53.6 And after this the Righteous and Chosen One will cause the house of his congregation to appear; from then on, in the name of the Lord of Spirits, they will not be hindered.

53.7 And in front of him these mountains will not be firm like the earth, and the hills will be like a spring of water; and the righteous will have rest from the ill-treatment of the sinners."

54.1 And I looked, and turned to another part of the Earth, and I saw there a deep valley with burning fire.

54.2 And they brought the kings and powerful and threw them into that valley.

54.3 And there my eyes saw how they made instruments for them - iron chains of immeasurable weight.

54.4 And I asked the Angel of Peace, who went with me, saying: "These chain instruments - for whom are they being prepared?"

54.5 And he said to me: "These are being prepared for the hosts of Azazel, so that they may take them, and throw them into the lowest part of hell; and they will cover their jaws with rough stones, as the Lord of Spirits commanded.

54.6 And Michael and Gabriel, Raphael and Phanuel - these will take hold of them on that great day. And throw them, on that day, into the furnace of burning fire, so that the Lord of Spirits may take vengeance on them for their iniquity, in that they became servants of Satan, and led astray those who dwell upon the dry ground.

54.7 And in those days, the punishment of the Lord of Spirits will go out, and all the storehouses of the waters which are above the sky and under the earth, will be opened.

54.8 And all the waters will be joined with the waters that are above the sky. The water that is above the sky is male and the water that is under the Earth is female.

54.9 And all those who dwell upon the dry ground, and those who dwell under the ends of Heaven, will be wiped out.

54.10 And because of this they will acknowledge their iniquity which they have committed on the Earth and through this they will be destroyed."

55.1 And after this, the Head of Days repented, and said:
"I have destroyed to no purpose all those who dwell upon the dry ground."

55.2 And he swore by His Great Name: "From now on I will not act like this towards all those who dwell upon the dry ground. And I will put a sign in Heaven, and it will be a pledge of faith between me and them forever, so long as Heaven is above the Earth.

55.3 And this will be in accordance with my command. When I want to take hold of them with the hands of the Angels, on the day of distress and pain, in the face of my anger and my wrath, my wrath and anger will remain upon them" says the Lord, The Lord of Spirits.

55.4 "You powerful kings who dwell upon the dry ground will be obliged to watch my Chosen One sit down on the throne of My Glory, and judge, in the Name of the Lord of Spirits, Azazel and all his associates and all his hosts."

56.1 And I saw there the hosts of the Angels of Punishment, as they went, and they were holding chains of iron and bronze.

56.2 And I asked the Angel of Peace, who went with me, saying: "To whom are those who are holding the chains going?"

56.3 And he said to me: "Each to his own chosen ones, and to their beloved ones, so that they may be thrown into the chasm, in the depths of the valley."

56.4 And then, that valley will be filled with their chosen and beloved ones, and the days of their life will be at an end, and the days of their leading astray will no longer be counted.

56.5 And in those days, the Angels will gather together, and will throw themselves towards the east, upon the Parthians and Medes. They will stir up the kings so that a disturbing spirit will come upon them, and they will drive them from their thrones; and they will come out like lions from their lairs, and like hungry wolves in the middle of their flocks.

56.6 And they will go up and trample on the Land of My Chosen Ones, and the land of my chosen ones will become before them a tramping-ground and a beaten track.

56.7 But the City of My Righteous Ones will be a hindrance to their horses, and they will stir up slaughter amongst themselves, and their own right hand will be strong against them. And a man will not admit to knowing his neighbour, or his brother, nor a son his father, or his mother, until, through their death, there are corpses enough; and their punishment - it will not be in vain.

56.8 And in those days Sheol will open its mouth and they will sink into it and their destruction; Sheol will swallow up the sinners in front of the faces of the chosen."

57.1 And it came to pass, after this, that I saw another host of chariots with men riding on them, and they came upon the wind from the east and from the west, to the south.

57.2 And the sound of the noise of their chariots was heard. And when this occurred the Holy Ones observed it from Heaven and the Pillars of the Earth were shaken from their foundations. And the sound was heard from the ends of the Earth to the ends of Heaven throughout one day.

57.3 And all will fall down and worship the Lord of Spirits. And this is the end of the second parable.

58.1 And I began to speak **The Third Parable**.
About The Righteous and about The Chosen.

58.2 Blessed are you, the righteous and the chosen, for your lot will be glorious!

58.3 And the righteous will be in the light of the Sun and the chosen in the light of eternal life. And there will be no end to the days of their life and the days of the Holy will be without number.

58.4 And they will seek the light and will find righteousness with the Lord of Spirits. Peace be to the righteous with the Lord of the World!

58.5 And after this it will be said to the Holy that they should seek in Heaven the secrets of righteousness, the lot of faith; for it has become bright as the Sun upon the dry ground, and darkness has passed away.

58.6 And there will be ceaseless light, and to a limit of days, they will not come, for darkness will have been destroyed previously. And the light will endure in front of the Lord of Spirits, and the light of uprightness will endure in front of the Lord of Spirits, forever.

59.1 And in those days my eyes saw the secrets of the flashes of lightning, and the lights, and the regulations governing them; and they flash for a blessing or a curse, as the Lord of Spirits wishes.

59.2 And there I saw the secrets of the thunder and how when it crashes in Heaven above the sound of it is heard. And they showed me the dwellings of the dry ground, and the sound of the thunder, for peace, and for blessing, or for a curse, according to the word of the Lord of Spirits.

59.3 And after this all the secrets of the lights, and of the flashes of lightning, were shown to me. They flash to bring blessing and satisfaction.

60.1 In the fiftieth year, in the seventh month, on the fourteenth day of the month of the life of Enoch. In that parable, I saw how the Heaven of Heavens was shaken violently, and the Host of the Most High and the Angels, a thousand thousands and ten thousand times ten thousand, were extremely disturbed.

60.2 And then I saw the Head of Days sitting on the throne of his glory and the Angels and righteous were sitting around him.

60.3 And a great trembling seized me, and fear took hold of me, and my loins collapsed and gave way, and my whole being melted, and I fell upon my face.

60.4 And the Holy Michael sent another Holy Angel, one of the Holy Angels, and he raised me; and when he raised me my spirit returned, for I had been unable to endure the sight of that host, and the disturbance, and the shaking of Heaven.

60.5 And the Holy Michael said to me: "What sight has disturbed you like this? Until today has the day of His mercy lasted and He has been merciful and long suffering towards those who dwell upon the dry ground.

60.6 And when the Day, and the Power, and the Punishment, and the Judgment come that the Lord of Spirits has prepared for those who worship the Righteous Judgment, and for those who deny the Righteous Judgment, and for those who take His name in vain - and that Day has been prepared. For the chosen a covenant, but for the sinners a visitation."

60.7 And on that day two monsters will be separated from one another, a female monster whose name is Leviathan, to dwell in the depths of the sea, above the springs of the waters.

60.8 And the name of the male is Behemoth who occupies with his breast an immense desert named Dendayn on the east of the Garden where the chosen and the righteous dwell. Where my great-grandfather was received, who was seventh from Adam, the first man whom the Lord of Spirits made.

60.9 And I asked that other Angel to show me the power of those monsters, how they were separated on one day, and thrown, one into the depths of the sea and the other on to the dry ground of the desert.

60.10 And he said to me: "Son of man, you here wish to know what is secret."

60.11 And the other Angel spoke to me, the one who went with me and showed me what is secret; what is first and last in Heaven, in the heights, and under the dry ground, in the depths, and at the Ends of Heaven, and at the Foundations of Heaven, and in the Storehouses of the Winds.

60.12 And how the spirits are distributed, and how they are weighed. And how the springs, and the winds, are counted according to the power of their spirit. And the power of the light of the Moon. And the divisions of the stars according to their names. And how all the divisions are made.

60.13 And the thunder - according to the places were it falls. And all the divisions that are made in lightning - so that it may flash. And its hosts - how they quickly obey.

60.14 For the thunder have fixed intervals, which have been given to its sound, for waiting. And the thunder and the lightning are not separate although not the same. Through a spirit the two of them move inseparably.

60.15 For when the lightning flashes the thunder utters its voice, and the spirit, at the proper time, causes it to rest, and divides equally between them because the storehouse of the times for their occurrence is like that of the sand. And each of them, at the proper time, is held by a rein, and turned back by the power of the spirit, and likewise driven forward, according to the number of the regions of the Earth.

60.16 And the spirit of the sea is male and strong, and according to the power of its strength, the spirit turns it back with a rein, and likewise it is driven forward, and scattered amongst all the mountains of the Earth.

60.17 And the spirit of the hoarfrost is its own Angel; and the spirit of the hail, is a good Angel.

60.18 And the spirit of the snow has withdrawn because of its power, and it has a special spirit, and that which rises from it is like smoke and its name is frost.

60.19 And the spirit of the mist is not associated with them in their storehouse but has a special storehouse; for its course is glorious both in light and darkness, and in winter and in summer, and its storehouse is an Angel.

60.20 The spirit of the dew has its dwelling at the ends of Heaven and is connected with the storehouses of the rain. And its course is in winter and in summer and its clouds. And the clouds of the mist are associated and one gives to the other.

60.21 And when the spirit of the rain moves from its storehouse the Angels come and open the storehouse and bring it out. And when it is scattered over all the dry ground it joins with all the water that is on the dry ground. And whenever it joins with the water that is on the dry ground.(......)

60.22 For the waters are for those who dwell upon the dry ground, for they are nourishment for the dry ground, from the Most High who is in Heaven.

Therefore there is a fixed measure for the rain and the Angels comprehend it.

60.23 All these things, I saw towards the Garden of Righteousness.

60.24 And the Angel of Peace who was with me, said to me: "These two monsters, prepared in accordance with the greatness of the Lord, will feed them that Punishment of the Lord. And children will be killed with their mothers and sons with their fathers.

60.25 When the punishment of the Lord of Spirits rests upon them it will remain resting so that the punishment of the Lord of Spirits may not come in vain upon these. Afterwards, the judgment will be according to His mercy and His patience."

61.1 And in those days, I saw long cords given to those Angels and they acquired wings for themselves, and flew, and went towards the north.

61.2 And I asked the Angel, saying: "Why did these take the long cords, and go?" And he said to me: "They went so that they may measure."

61.3 And the Angel who went with me, said to me:

"These will bring the measurements of the righteous, and the ropes of the righteous, to the righteous, that they may rely on the name of the Lord of Spirits for ever and ever.

61.4 The chosen will begin to dwell with the chosen, and these measurements will be given to faith, and will strengthen righteousness.

61.5 And these measurements will reveal all the secrets of the depths of the Earth, and those who were destroyed by the desert, and those who were devoured by the fish of the sea, and by

animals, that they may return and rely on the Day of the Chosen One. For no one will be destroyed in front of the Lord of Spirits, and no one can be destroyed."

61.6 And all those in the Heavens above received a command, and power, and one voice, and one light like fire was given to them.

61.7 And Him, before everything, they blessed, and exalted, and praised in wisdom. And they showed themselves wise in speech and in the spirit of life.

61.8 And the Lord of Spirits set the Chosen One on the throne of his glory, and he will judge all the works of the Holy ones in Heaven above, and in the Balance he will weigh their deeds.

61.9 And when he lifts his face to judge their secret ways according to the word of the name of the Lord of Spirits, and their path according to the way of the Righteous Judgment of the Lord Most High, they will all speak with one voice and bless, and praise, and exalt, and glorify, the Name of the Lord of Spirits.

61.10 And he will call all the Host of the Heavens and all the Holy Ones above, and the Host of the Lord, the Cherubim, and the Seraphim, and the Ophannim, and all the Angels of Power, and all the Angels of the Principalities, and the Chosen One, and the other host that is upon the dry ground, and over the water, on that Day.

61.11 And they will raise one voice, and will bless, and praise, and glorify, and exalt, in the spirit of faith, and in the spirit of wisdom, and of patience, and in the spirit of mercy, and in the spirit of justice, and of peace, and in the spirit of goodness. And they will all say with one voice: "Blessed is He, and blessed be the name of the Lord of Spirits for ever and ever."

61.12 All Those Who Do Not Sleep in Heaven above will bless him. All His Holy Ones who are in Heaven, will bless Him, and all the chosen ones who dwell in the Garden of Life, and every spirit able to bless, and praise and exalt, and hallow your Holy Name. And all flesh which to the limit of its power, will praise, and bless, your Name forever and ever.

61.13 For great is the mercy of the Lord of Spirits, and he is long-suffering; and all his works and all his forces, as many as he has made, he has revealed to the righteous and the chosen, in the Name of the Lord of Spirits.

62.1 And thus the Lord commanded the kings, and the mighty and the exalted, and those who dwell upon the earth, and said: "Open your eyes and raise your horns if you are able to acknowledge the Chosen One."

62.2 And the Lord of Spirits sat on His Throne of Glory, and the spirit of righteousness was poured out on him, and the word of his mouth kills all the sinners and all the lawless, and they are destroyed in front of him.

62.3 And on that Day, all the kings and the mighty and the exalted, and those who possess the earth, will stand up and they will see and recognize how he sits on the Throne of His Glory. And the righteous are judged in righteousness, in front of him, and no idle word is spoken in front of him.

62.4 And pain will come upon them as upon a woman in labour, for whom giving birth is difficult when her child enters the mouth of the womb, and she has difficulty giving birth.

62.5 And one half of them will look at the other, and they will be terrified, and will cast down their faces, and pain will take hold of them when they see that son of a woman sitting on the throne of His Glory.

62.6 And the mighty kings, and all those who possess the earth, will praise and bless and exalt Him who rules everything that is hidden.

62.7 For from the beginning that Son of Man was hidden, and the Most High kept him in the presence of His power, and revealed him only to the chosen.

62.8 And the community of the Holy and the chosen will be sown and all the chosen will stand before him on that day.

62.9 And all the mighty kings, and the exalted, and those who rule the dry ground, will fall down before him, on their faces, and worship; and they will set their hopes on that Son of Man, and will entreat him, and will petition for mercy from him.

62.10 But the Lord of Spirits will then so press them that they will hasten to go out from before Him, and their faces will be filled with shame, and the darkness will grow deeper on their faces.

62.11 And the Angels of Punishment will take them so that they may repay them for the wrong that they did to His children and to His chosen ones.

62.12 And they will become a spectacle to the righteous and to His chosen ones; they will rejoice over them, for the anger of the Lord of Spirits will rest upon them, and the sword of the Lord of Spirits will be drunk with them.

62.13 And the righteous and the chosen will be saved on that Day and they will never see the faces of the sinners and the lawless from then on.

62.14 And the Lord of Spirits will remain over them and with that Son of Man they will dwell, and eat, and lie down, and rise up, forever and ever.

62.15 And the righteous and chosen will have risen from the earth, and will have ceased to cast down their faces, and will have put on the Garment of Life.

62.16 And this will be a Garment of Life from the Lord of Spirits; and your garments will not wear out, and your glory will not fail, in front of the Lord of Spirits.

63.1 In those days, the mighty kings who possess the dry ground will entreat the Angels of His Punishment to whom they have been handed over so that they might give them a little respite. And so that they might fall down and worship in front of the Lord of Spirits, and confess their sins in front of Him.

63.2 And they will bless and praise the Lord of Spirits, and say: "Blessed be the Lord of Spirits, and the Lord of Kings, the Lord of the Mighty, and the Lord of the Rich, and the Lord of Glory, and the Lord of Wisdom!

63.3 And everything secret is clear, in front of You, and your power is for all generations, and your glory is forever and ever. Deep and without number are all your secrets and your righteousness is beyond reckoning.

63.4 Now we realize that we ought to praise and bless the Lord of Kings and the one who is King over all Kings."

63.5 And they will say: "Would that we might be given a respite, so that we might praise and thank and bless him, and make our confession in front of His Glory.

63.6 And now we long for a respite, but do not find it; we are driven off and do not obtain it; and the light has passed away from before us, and darkness will be our dwelling forever and ever.

63.7 For we have not made our confession before him, and we have not praised the name of the Lord of Kings, and we have not praised the Lord for all his works, but our hopes have been on the sceptre of our kingdom, and of our glory.

63.8 And on the day of our affliction and distress he does not save us, and we find no respite to make our confession that our Lord is faithful in all his doings, and in all his judgments and his justice, and that his judgments show no respect for persons.

63.9 And we pass away from in front of him because of all our works and all our sins have been counted exactly."

63.10 Then they will say to them: "Our souls are sated with possessions gained through iniquity, but they do not prevent our going down into the flames of the torment of Sheol."

63.11 And after this their faces will be filled with darkness and shame, in front of that Son of Man, and they will be driven away from him. And the sword will dwell among them - in front of Him.

63.12 And thus says the Lord of Spirits: "This is the Law and the Judgment for the mighty, and the kings, and the exalted, and for those who possess the dry ground, in front of the Lord of Spirits."

64.1 And I saw other figures hidden in that place.

64.2 I heard the voice of the Angel saying: "These are the Angels who came down from Heaven onto the Earth and revealed what is secret to the sons of men, and led astray the sons of men, so that they committed sin."

65.1 And in those days, Noah saw the Earth had tilted and that its destruction was near.

65.2 And he set off from there and went to the ends of the Earth and cried out to his great-grandfather Enoch; and Noah said three times in a bitter voice: "Hear me, hear me, hear me!"

65.3 And he said to him: "Tell me, what is it that is being done on the Earth, that the Earth is so afflicted and shaken, lest I be destroyed with it!"

65.4 And immediately there was a great disturbance on the Earth and a voice was heard from Heaven and I fell upon my face.

65.5 And my great-grandfather Enoch came, stood by me, and said to me: "Why did you cry out to me, with such bitter crying and weeping?

65.6 And a command has gone out from the Lord against those who dwell upon the dry ground that this must be their end. For they have learnt all the secrets of the Angels, and all the wrongdoings of the satans, and all their secret power, and all the power of those who practice magic arts, and the power of enchantments, and the power of those who cast molten images for all the Earth.

65.7 And further, how silver is produced from the dust of the earth and how soft metal occurs on the earth.

65.8 For lead and tin are not produced from the earth, like the former; there is a spring which produces them, and an Angel who stands in it, and that Angel distributes them."

65.9 And after this, my great grandfather Enoch took hold of me with his hand, and raised me, and said to me: "Go, for I have asked the Lord of Spirits about this disturbance on the earth." **65.10** And he said to me: "Because of their iniquity, their judgment has been completed, and they will no longer be counted before me; because of the sorceries they have searched out and learnt, the Earth and those who dwell upon it will be destroyed.

65.11 And for these, there will be no place of refuge, for ever, for they showed to them what is secret, and they have been condemned; but not so for you, my son; the Lord of Spirits knows that you are pure and innocent of this reproach concerning the secrets.

65.12 And he has established your name among the Holy, and will keep you from amongst those who dwell upon the dry ground; and he has destined your offspring in righteousness, to be kings, and for great honours. And from your offspring will flow out a spring of the Righteous and Holy, without number forever."

66.1 And after this, he showed me the Angels of Punishment, who were ready to come and release all the forces of the water, which is under the earth, in order to bring judgment and destruction on all those who reside and dwell upon the dry ground.

66.2 And the Lord of Spirits commanded the Angels who were coming out, not to raise their hands, but to keep watch; for those Angels were in charge of the forces of the waters.

66.3 And I came out from before Enoch.

67.1 And in those days, the word of the Lord came to me, and he said to me: "Noah, behold; your lot has come up before me, a lot without reproach, a lot of love and uprightness.

67.2 And now the Angels are making a wooden structure, and when the Angels come out from that task, I will put my hand on it, and keep it safe. And a change shall take place so that the dry ground may not remain empty.

67.3 And I will establish your offspring before me, forever and ever, and I will scatter those who dwell with you, over the face of the dry ground. I will not again put them to the test, on the face of the Earth, but they will be blessed and increase on the dry ground in the name of the Lord."

67.4 And they will shut up those Angels, who showed iniquity, in that burning valley, which my greatgrandfather Enoch had shown to me previously, in the west, near the mountains of gold and silver and iron and soft metal and tin.

67.5 And I saw that valley, in which there was a great disturbance, and a heaving of the waters.

67.6 And when all this happened, from the fiery molten metal, and the disturbance, which disturbed the waters in that place, a smell of sulphur was produced, and it was associated with those waters. And that valley of the Angels, who led men astray, burns under the ground.

67.7 And through the valleys of that same area, flow out rivers of fire where those Angels will be punished, who led astray those on the dry ground.

67.8 And in those days, those waters will serve the kings, and the mighty, and the exalted, and those who dwell upon dry ground, for the healing of soul and body, but also for the punishment of the spirit. And their spirits are so full of lust that they will be punished in their bodies, for they denied the Lord of Spirits. And they see their punishment every day yet they do not believe in His Name.

67.9 And the more their bodies are burnt, the more a change will come over their spirits, for ever and ever; for no one can speak an idle word in front of the Lord of Spirits.

67.10 For judgment will come upon them, for they believe in the lust of their bodies, but deny the spirit of the Lord.

67.11 And those same waters will undergo a change in those days; for when those Angels are punished in those days, the temperature of those springs of water will change, and when the

Angels come up, that water of the springs will change, and become cold.

67.12 And I heard the Holy Michael answering and saying: "This judgment, with which the Angels are judged, is a testimony for the kings and the mighty who possess the dry ground.

67.13 For these waters of judgment serve for the healing of the bodies of the kings, and for the lust of their bodies; but they do not see, and do not believe, that these waters will change, and will become a fire which burns forever."

68.1 And after this, my greatgrandfather Enoch gave me the explanation of all the secrets, in a book, and the parables that had been given to him; and he put them together for me, in the words of the Book of Parables.

68.2 And on that day the Holy Michael answered Raphael, saying: "The power of the spirit seizes me and makes me tremble because of the harshness of the judgment of the Angels. Who can endure the harshness of the judgment which has been executed and before which they melt with fear?"

68.3 And the Holy Michael answered Raphael again, and said to him: "Who would not soften his heart over it, and whose mind would not be disturbed by this word? Judgment has gone out against them, upon those whom they have led out like this."

68.4 But it came to pass, when he stood before the Lord of Spirits, that the Holy Michael spoke as follows to Raphael: "I will not take their part under the eye of the Lord, for the Lord of Spirits is angry with them, because they act as if they were the Lord.

68.5 Because of this the hidden judgment will come upon them for ever and ever; for neither any other Angel, nor any man, will receive their lot, but they alone have received their judgment for ever and ever.

69.1 And after this judgment I will terrify them, and make them tremble, for they have shown this to those who dwell upon the dry ground."

69.2 And behold, the names of those Angels: - The first of them is **Semyaza (Azza)**, and the second **Artaqifa**, and the third **Armen**, and the fourth Kokabiel, and the fifth Turiel, and the sixth Ramiel, and the seventh Daniel, and the eighth Nuqael, and the ninth **Baraqiel**, and the tenth **Azazel**, and the eleventh **Armaros**, the twelfth **Batriel**, the thirteenth **Basasael**, the fourteenth **Ananel**, the fifteenth **Turiel**, the sixteenth **Samsiel**, the seventeenth **Yetarel**, the eighteenth **Tumiel**, the nineteenth **Turiel**, the twentieth **Rumiel**, the twenty-first **Azazel**.

69.3 And these are the chiefs of their Angels, and the names of the leaders of hundreds, and their leaders of fifties, and their leaders of tens.

69.4 The name of the first is Yequn; this is the one who led astray all the children of the Holy Angels, and he brought them down onto the dry ground, and led them astray through the daughters of men.

69.5 And the name of the second is Asbeel; this one suggested an evil plan to the children of the Holy Angels, and led them astray, so that they corrupted their bodies with the daughters of men. **69.6** And the name of the third is Gadreel; this is the one that showed all the deadly blows to the sons of men. And he led astray Eve. And he showed the weapons of death to the children of men, the shield and the breastplate, and the sword for slaughter, and all the weapons of death to the sons of men.

69.7 And from his hand they have gone out against those who dwell the dry ground from that time and forever and ever.

69.8 And the name of the fourth is Penemue; this one showed the sons of men the bitter and the sweet and showed them all the secrets of their wisdom.

69.9 He taught men the art of writing with ink and paper, and through this many have gone astray, from eternity to eternity, and to this day.

69.10 For men were not created for this, that they should confirm their faith like this, with pen and ink.

69.11 For men were created no differently from the Angels, so that they might remain righteous and pure, and death, which destroys everything, would not have touched them; but through this knowledge of theirs they are being destroyed and through this power death consumes them. **69.12** And the name of the fifth is Kasdeyae; this one showed the sons of men all the evil blows of the spirits and of the demons, and the blows that attack the embryo in the womb so that it miscarries. And the blows that attack the soul: the bite of the serpent. And the blows that occur at midday, and the son of the serpent - who is strong.

69.13 And this is the task of Kesbeel, the chief of the oath, who showed the oath to the Holy ones when he dwelt on high in glory. And his name is Beqa.

69.14 And this one told the Holy Michael that he should show him the secret name so that they might mention it in the oath, so that those, who showed the sons of men everything that is secret, trembled before that name and oath.

69.15 And this is the power of this oath, for it is powerful and strong, and he placed this oath, Akae, in the charge of the Holy Michael.

69.16 And these are the secrets of this oath, and they are strong through this oath, and Heaven was suspended, before the world was created, and forever. **69.17** And through it the earth was founded upon the water, and from the hidden recesses of the mountains come beautiful waters, from the creation of the world and for ever.

69.18 And through that oath the sea was created, and as its foundation, for the time of anger, he placed for it the sand, and it does not go beyond it, from the creation of the world and for ever.

69.19 And through that oath the deeps were made firm, and they stand and do not move from their place, from the creation of the world and for ever.

69.20 And through that oath the Sun and the Moon complete their course and do not transgress their command, from the creation of the world and for ever.

69.21 And through that oath the stars complete their course, and he calls their names, and they answer him, from the creation of the world and for ever.

69.22 And likewise the spirits of the water, of the winds, and of all the breezes, and their paths, according to all the groups of the spirits.

69.23 And there are kept the store-houses of the sound of thunder, and of the light of the lightning; and there are kept the storehouses of the hail, and the hoarfrost, and the storehouses of the mist, and the storehouses of the rain and dew.

69.24 And all these make their confession and give thanks in front of the Lord of Spirits and sing praises with all their power. And their food consists of all their thanksgiving and they give thanks, praise, and exalt, in the name of the Lord of Spirits, forever and ever.

69.25 And this oath is strong over them and through it they are kept safe and their courses are not disturbed.

69.26 And they had great joy and they blessed, praised, and exalted, because the name of that Son of Man had been revealed to them. **69.27** And he sat on the Throne of His Glory and the whole judgment was given to the Son of Man and he will cause the sinners to pass away and be destroyed from the face of the Earth. **69.28** And those who led astray the world will be bound in chains and will be shut up in the assembly-place of their destruction, and all their works will pass away from the face of the earth.

69.29 And from then on there will be nothing corruptible. For that Son of Man has appeared, and has sat on the Throne of His Glory, and everything evil will pass away and go from in front of Him; and the word of that Son of Man will be strong in front of the Lord of Spirits.

This is the Third Parable of Enoch.

70

.1 And it came to pass, after this, that while he was living his name was lifted from those who dwell upon the dry ground to the presence of that Son of Man, and to the presence of the Lord of Spirits.

70.2 And he was lifted on the chariots of the spirit, and his name vanished from among them.

70.3 And from that day I was not counted among them, and He placed me between two winds, between the north and the west, where the Angels took the cords to measure for me the place for the chosen and the righteous.

70.4 And there I saw the First Fathers and the righteous who from the beginning of the world dwelt in that place.

71

.1 And it came to pass, after this, that my spirit was carried off, and it went up into the Heavens. I saw the sons of the Holy Angels treading upon flames of fire their garments were white, and their clothing, and the light of their face, was like snow.

71.2 And I saw two rivers of fire, and the light of that fire shone like a hyacinth, and I fell upon my face in front of the Lord of Spirits.

71.3 And the Angel Michael, one of the Archangels, took hold of me by my right hand, and raised me and led me out to all the secrets of mercy, and the secrets of righteousness.

71.4 And he showed me all the secrets of the Ends of Heaven and all the Storehouses of the Stars and the

Lights from where they come out from below the Holy Ones.

71.5 And the Spirit carried Enoch off to the Highest Heaven, and I saw there, in the middle of that Light, something built of crystal stones, and in the middle of those stones tongues of living fire.

71.6 And my spirit saw a circle of fire, which surrounded that house; from its four sides came rivers, full of living fire, and they surrounded that house.

71.7 And round about were the Seraphim and the Cherubim, and the Ophannim; these are They Who Do Not Sleep but keep watch over the Throne of His Glory.

71.8 And I saw Angels, who could not be counted, a thousand thousands and ten thousand times ten thousand, surrounding that house. And Michael, and Raphael, and Gabriel, and Phanuel, and the Holy Angels who are in the Heavens above, went in and out of that house.

71.9 And Michael, and Raphael, and Gabriel, and Phanuel, and many Holy Angels without number, came out from that house.

71.10 And with them the Head of Days, his head white, and pure, like wool and his garments - indescribable.

71.11 And I fell upon my face, and my whole body melted, and my spirit was transformed; and I cried out in a loud voice, in the spirit of power, and I blessed, praised, and exalted.

71.12 And these blessings, which came out from my mouth, were pleasing before that Head of Days.

71.13 And that Head of Days came with Michael, Gabriel, Raphael and Phanuel, and thousands and tens of thousands of Angels without number.

71.14 And that Angel, came to me, and greeted me with his voice, and said to me: "You are the son of man who was born to righteousness and righteousness remains over you and the righteousness of the Head of Days, will not leave you."

71.15 And he said to me: "He proclaims peace to you in the name of the world which is to come, for from there peace has come out from the creation of the world and so you will have it for ever and for ever and ever.

71.16 And all will walk according to your way, inasmuch as righteousness will never leave you. With you will be their dwelling, and with you their lot, and they will not be separated from you for ever and for ever and ever.

71.17 And so there will be length of days with that Son of Man, and the righteous will have peace, and the righteous will have an upright way in the name of the Lord of Spirits, for ever and ever."

SECTION III.
CHAPTERS LXXII-LXXXII
THE BOOK OF THE
HEAVENLY LUMINARIES

72.1 The Book of the Revolutions of the Lights of Heaven.

Each as it is, according to their classes, according to their period of rule and their times, according to their names and places of origin, and according to their months. That Uriel, the Holy Angel who was with me, and is their leader, showed to me. And he showed me all their regulations, exactly as they are, for each year of the world and for ever, until the new creation shall be made which will last forever.

72.2 And this is the First Law of the Lights. The light called the Sun; its rising is in the Gates of Heaven that are towards the east, and its setting is in the western Gates of Heaven.

72.3 And I saw six Gates from which the Sun rises, and six Gates in which the Sun sets, and the Moon also rises and sets in those Gates, and the leaders of the stars together with those whom they lead. There are six in the east and six in the west, all exactly in place, one next to the other; and there are many windows to the south and the north of those Gates.

72.4 And first there rises the greater light, named the Sun, and its disc is like the disc of Heaven, and the whole of it is full of a fire which gives light and warmth.

72.5 The wind blows the chariots on which it ascends, and the Sun goes down in the sky and returns through the north in order to reach the east, and is led so that it comes to the appropriate Gate and shines in the sky.

72.6 In this way it rises in the first month, in the large Gate, namely; it rises through the fourth of those six Gates that are towards the east.

72.7 And in that fourth Gate, through which the Sun rises in the first month, there are twelve window-openings from which, whenever they are opened, flames come out.

72.8 When the Sun rises in Heaven it goes out through that fourth Gate for thirty days, and exactly in the fourth Gate, in the west of Heaven, it goes down.

72.9 And in those days the day grows daily longer, and the night grows nightly shorter, until the thirtieth morning.

72.10 And on that day the day becomes longer than the night by a double part, and the day amounts to exactly ten parts, and the night amounts to eight parts.

72.11 And the Sun rises from that fourth Gate, and sets in the fourth Gate, and returns to the fifth Gate in the east for thirty mornings; and it rises from it and sets in the fifth Gate.

72.12 And then the day becomes longer by two parts, and the day amounts to eleven parts, and the night becomes shorter and amounts to seven parts.

72.13 And the Sun returns to the east and comes to the sixth Gate, and rises and sets in the sixth Gate for thirty-one mornings, because of its sign.

72.14 And on that day the day becomes longer than the night, and the day becomes double the night; and the day amounts to twelve parts, and the night becomes shorter and amounts to six parts.

72.15 And the Sun rises up so that the day may grow shorter, and the night longer; and the Sun returns to the east, and comes to the sixth Gate, and rises from it, and sets, for thirty mornings.

72.16 And when thirty mornings have been completed the day becomes shorter, by exactly one part; and the day amounts to eleven parts, and the night to seven parts.

72.17 And the Sun goes out from the west, through that sixth Gate, and goes to the east, and rises in the fifth Gate for thirty mornings and it sets in the west again, in the fifth Gate in the west.

72.18 On that day the day becomes shorter by two parts, and the day amounts to ten parts, and the night to eight parts.

72.19 And the Sun rises from that fifth Gate, and sets in the fifth Gate in the west, and rises in the fourth Gate for thirty-one mornings because of its sign, and sets in the west.

72.20 On that day the day becomes equal with the night, and is of equal length; and the night amounts to nine parts, and the day to nine parts.

72.21 And the Sun rises from that Gate and sets in the west, and returns to the east, and rises in the third Gate for thirty mornings, and sets in the west in the third Gate.

72.22 And the Sun rises from that third Gate, and sets in the third Gate in the west, and returns to the east; and the Sun rises in the second Gate in the east for thirty mornings, and likewise, it sets in the second Gate, in the west of Heaven.

72.24 And on that day the night amounts to eleven parts and the day to seven parts.

72.25 And the Sun rises, on that day, from the second Gate, and sets in the west in the second Gate, and returns to the east to the first Gate for thirty-one mornings, then sets in the west in the first Gate.

72.26 And on that day the night becomes longer, and becomes double the day; and the night amounts to exactly twelve parts, and the day to six parts.

72.27 And with this, the Sun has completed the divisions of its journey, and it turns back again, along these divisions of its journey; and it comes through that first Gate for thirty mornings, and sets in the west opposite it.

72.28 And on that day the night becomes shorter in length by one part, and amounts to eleven parts, and the day to seven parts.

72.29 And the Sun returns, and comes to the second Gate in the east, and it returns along those divisions of its journey for thirty mornings, rising and setting.

72.30 And on that day the night becomes shorter in length and the night amounts to ten parts and the day to eight parts.

72.31 And on that day, the Sun rises from the second Gate, and sets in the west, and returns to the east, and rises in the third Gate for thirty one mornings, and sets in the west of the sky.

72.32 And on that day the night becomes shorter, and amounts to nine parts, and the day amounts to nine parts, and the night becomes equal with the day. And the year amounts to exactly **364** days.

72.33 And the length of the day and the night, and the shortness of the day and the night - they are different because of the journey of the Sun.

72.34 Because of it, its journey becomes daily longer, and nightly shorter.

72.35 And this is the law and the journey of the Sun and its return, as often as it returns; sixty times it returns and rises, that is the great eternal light, which for ever and ever is named the Sun.

72.36 And this that rises is the great light, which is named after its appearance, as the Lord commanded.

72.37 And thus it rises and sets; it neither decreases, nor rests, but runs day and night in its chariot. And its light is seven times brighter than that of the Moon but in size the two are equal.

73.1 And after this law I saw another law, for the lesser light, named the Moon.

73.2 And its disc is like the disc of the Sun, and the wind blows its chariot on which it rides, and in fixed measure light is given to it.

73.3 And every month it's rising and setting change, and its days are as the days of the Sun, and when its light is uniformly full, it is a seventh part the light of the Sun.

73.4 And thus it rises, and its first phase is towards the east; it rises on the thirtieth morning. And on that day it appears, and becomes for you the first phase of the Moon, on the thirtieth morning, together with the Sun in the Gate through which the Sun rises.

73.5 And a half.(.....) .with a seventh part, and its entire disc is empty, without light, except for a seventh part, a fourteenth part of it's light.

73.6 And on the day that it receives a seventh part and a half of its light, its light amounts to a seventh, and a seventh part and a half.

73.7 It sets with the Sun, and when the Sun rises, the Moon rises with it, and receives a half of one part of light. And on that night at the beginning of its morning, at the beginning of the Moon's day, the Moon sets with the Sun, and is dark on that night in six and seven parts and a half.

73.8 And it rises on that day, with exactly a seventh part, goes out, recedes from the rising of the Sun, and becomes bright on the remainder of its days, in the other six and seven parts.

74.1 And another journey, and law, I saw for it, in that according to this law it makes its monthly journey.

74.2 And Uriel, the Holy Angel who is leader of them all, showed me everything, and I wrote down their positions as he showed them to me. And I wrote down their months, as they are, and the appearance of their light, until fifteen days have been completed.

74.3 In seventh parts it makes all its darkness full, and in seventh parts it makes all its light full, in the east and in the west.

74.4 And in certain months, it changes its setting, and in certain months, it follows its own individual course.

74.5 In two months it sets with the Sun, in those two Gates that are in the middle, in the third and in the fourth Gate.

74.6 It goes out for seven days and turns back, and returns again to the Gate from which the Sun rises. And in that Gate it makes all its light full, and it recedes from the Sun, and comes, in eight days, to the sixth Gate from which the Sun rises.

74.7 And when the Sun rises from the fourth Gate, the Moon goes out for seven days, until it rises from the fifth Gate. And again it returns in seven days to the fourth Gate, makes all its light full, recedes, and comes to the first Gate in eight days.

74.8 And again it returns in seven days to the fourth Gate from which the Sun rises.

74.9 Thus I saw their positions; how the Moon rose and the Sun set in those days.

74.10 And if five years are added together, the Sun has an excess of thirty days. For each year, of the five years, there are three hundred and sixty four days.

74.11 And the excess, of the Sun and the stars, comes to six days. In five years, with six days each, they have an excess of thirty days, and the Moon falls behind the Sun and the stars by thirty days.

74.12 And the Moon conducts the years exactly, all of them according to their eternal positions; they are neither early nor late, even by one day, but change the year in exactly 364 days.

74.13 In three years, there are 1,092 days, and in five years 1,820 days, so that in eight years there are 2,912 days.

74.14 For the Moon alone, the days in three years come to 1,062 days, and in five years it is fifty days behind.

74.15 And there are 1,770 days in five years so that for the Moon the days in eight years amount to 2,832 days.

74.16 For the difference in eight years is eighty days, and all the days that the Moon is behind, in eight years, are eighty days.

74.17 And the year is completed exactly, in accordance with their positions, and the positions of the Sun, in that they rise from the Gates from which the Sun rises and sets for thirty days.

75.1 And the leaders of the tens of thousands, who are in charge of the whole of creation, and in charge of all the stars, and also the four days which are added, and are not separated from their position, according to the whole reckoning of the year. And these serve on the four days that are not counted in the reckoning of the year.

75.2 And because of them men go wrong in them. For these lights really serve in the stations of the world, one in the first Gate, and one in the third Gate, and one in the fourth Gate, and one in the sixth Gate. And the exact harmony of the world is completed in the separate 364 stations of the world.

75.3 For the signs, and the times, and the years, and the days, were showed to me by the Angel Uriel whom the Lord of Eternal Glory has placed in charge of all the Lights of Heaven. In Heaven and in the world, so that they might rule on the Face of Heaven, and appear over the earth, and be leaders of day and night; the Sun, the Moon, the stars, and all the serving creatures who revolve in all the Chariots of Heaven.

75.4 Likewise, Uriel showed to me twelve Gate-openings in the disc of the chariot of the Sun, in the sky, from which the rays of the Sun come out. And from them heat comes out over the Earth when they are opened at the times that are appointed for them.

75.5 And there are openings for the winds, and for the spirit of the dew, when they are opened at their times, opened in Heaven, at the ends of the earth.

75.6 I saw twelve Gates in Heaven, at the ends of the earth, from which the Sun, and the Moon, and the stars, and all the works of Heaven, go out in the east and in the west.

75.7 And there are many windowopenings to the north and to the south, and each window, at its appointed time, sends out heat corresponding to those Gates, from which the stars go out, in accordance with His command to them, and in which they set according to their number.

75.8 And I saw chariots in Heaven, running through the region above those Gates, in which the stars that never set rotate.

75.9 And one is bigger than all the others. And it goes round through the whole world.

76.1 And at the ends of the earth, I saw twelve Gates open to all the winds, from which the winds come out and blow over the earth.

76.2 Three of them open in the front of Heaven, and three in the back, and three on the right of Heaven, and three on the left.

76.3 And the three first are those towards the east, and then the three towards the north, and the three after these towards the south, and the three in the west.

76.4 Through four of them come winds of blessing and peace. And from the other eight come winds of punishment; when they are sent they bring devastation to the whole Earth, and to the water which is on it, and to all those who dwell upon it, and to everything that is in the water and on dry ground.

76.5 And the first wind from those Gates, called the east wind, comes out through the first Gate, which is towards the east. The one that comes from the south brings devastation, drought, heat, and destruction.

76.6 And through the second Gate, in the middle, comes what is right. And from it come rain, and fruitfulness, and prosperity, and dew. And through the third Gate, which is towards the north, comes cold and drought.

76.7 And after these, the winds towards the south come out, through three Gates. First, through the first of the Gates, which inclines towards the east, comes a hot wind.

76.8 And through the middle Gate, which is next to it, come pleasant fragrances, and dew, and rain, and prosperity, and life.

76.9 And through the third Gate, which is towards the west, come dew, and rain, and locusts, and devastation.

76.10 And after these, the winds towards the north..(...)..from the seventh Gate, which is towards the east, come dew and rain, locusts and devastation.

76.11 And through the Gate exactly in the middle, come rain, and dew, and life, and prosperity. And through the third Gate, which is towards the west come mist and hoarfrost, and snow, and rain, and dew, and locusts.

76.12 And after these the winds towards the west. Through the first Gate, which inclines towards the north, come dew, and rain, and hoarfrost, and cold, and snow, and frost.

76.13 And from the middle Gate, come dew and rain, prosperity and blessing. And through the last Gate, which is towards the south, come drought and devastation, burning and destruction.

76.14 And thus the twelve Gates, of the four quarters of Heaven are complete. And all their laws, and all their punishments, and all their benefits, I have shown to you, my son Methuselah.

77.1 They called the first quarter eastern because it is the first, and they call the second the south because there the Most High descends, and there especially the one who is blessed forever descends.

77.2 And the western quarter is called waning because there all the lights of Heaven wane and go down.

77.3 And the fourth quarter, named the north, is divided into three parts. And the first of them is the dwelling place for men; and the second contains seas of water, and the deeps, and the forests, and rivers, and darkness and mist; and the third part contains the Garden of Righteousness.

77.4 I saw seven high mountains, which were higher than all other mountains on the earth; and from them snow comes. And days and times and years, pass away and go by.

77.5 I saw seven rivers on the earth, larger than all the other rivers; one of them comes from the east and pours out its waters into the Great Sea.

77.6 And two of them come from the north to the sea and pour out their water into the Erythraean Sea in the east.

77.7 And the remaining four flow out on the side of the north, to their seas, two to the Erythraean Sea, and two into the Great Sea, and they discharge themselves there, and not into the wilderness, as some say.

77.8 I saw seven large islands, in the sea and on the land, two on the land, and five in the Great Sea.

78.1 The names of the Sun are as follows: The first Oryares, and the second Tomases.

78.2 The Moon has four names: The first name is Asonya, and the second Ebla, and the third Benase, and the fourth Era'e.

78.3 These are the two great lights; their disc is like the disc of Heaven and in size the two are equal.

78.4 In the disc of the Sun, are seven parts of light, which are added to it more than to the Moon, and in fixed measure light is transferred to the Moon until a seventh part of the Sun is exhausted.

78.5 And they set, go into the Gates of the west, go round through the north, and rise through the Gates of the east, on the face of Heaven.

78.6 And when the Moon rises, it appears in the sky, and has a half of a seventh part of light, and on the fourteenth day it makes all its light full.

78.7 And fifteen parts of light are transferred to it, until on the fifteenth day its light is full, according to the sign of the year, and amounts to fifteen parts. And the Moon comes into being by halves of a seventh part.

78.8 And in its waning on the first day, it decreases to fourteen parts of its light. And on the second to thirteen parts, and on the third to twelve parts, on the fourth to eleven parts, and on the fifth to ten parts, and on the sixth to nine parts, and on the seventh to eight parts, and on the eighth to seven parts, and on the ninth to six parts, and on the tenth to five parts, and on the eleventh to four parts, and on the twelfth to three, and on the thirteenth to two, and on the fourteenth to half of a seventh part. And all the light that remains from the total disappears on the fifteenth day.

78.9 And in certain months the Moon has twenty-nine days and once twenty-eight.

78.10 And Uriel showed me another law: - when light is transferred to the Moon, and on which side it is transferred from the Sun.

78.11 All the time that the Moon is increasing in its light, it transfers as it becomes opposite the Sun, until in fourteen days it's light is full in the sky; and when it is all ablaze, it's light is full in the sky.

78.12 And on the first day it is called the New Moon, for on that, daylight rises on it.

78.13 And its light becomes full exactly on the day that as the Sun goes down in the west it rises from the east for the night. And the Moon shines for the whole night until the Sun rises opposite it, and the Moon is seen opposite the Sun.

78.14 And on the side on which the light of the Moon appears, there again it wanes, until all its light disappears, and the days of the Moon end and its disc remains empty without light.

78.15 And for three months, at its proper time, it achieves thirty days, and for three months, it achieves twenty-nine days, during which it completes its waning, in the first period, in the first Gate, 127 days.

78.16 And in the time of it's rising, for three months, it appears in each month with thirty days. And for three months it appears in each month with twenty-nine days

78.17 By night, for twenty days each time, it looks like a man, and by day like Heaven, for there is nothing else in it except it's light.

79.1 And now, my son Methuselah, I have shown you everything, and the whole Law of the Stars of Heaven is complete.

79.2 And he showed me the whole law for these, for every day, and for every time, and for every rule, and for every year, and for the end thereof, according to its command, for every month and every week.

79.3 And the waning of the Moon, which occurs in the sixth Gate, for in that sixth Gate it's light becomes full, and after that it is the beginning of the month.

79.4 And the waning, which occurs in the first Gate, at its proper time, until 127 days are complete, or by weeks; twenty-five weeks and two days.

79.5 And how it falls behind the Sun, according to the law of the stars, by exactly five days in one period of time, when it has completed the pathway you have seen.

79.6 Such is the appearance, and likeness, of every light, which Uriel, the great Angel who is their leader, showed to me.

80.1 And in those days Uriel answered me and said to me: "Behold, I have shown you everything, Oh Enoch. And I have revealed everything to you, so that you may see this Sun, and this Moon, and those who lead the Stars of Heaven, and all those who turn them, their tasks and their times and their rising.

80.2 But in the days of the sinners the years will become shorter, and their seed will be late on their land, and on their fields. And all things on the earth will change and will not appear at their proper time. And the rain will be withheld and Heaven will retain it.

80.3 And in those times the fruits of the earth will be late, and will not grow at their proper time, and the fruits of the trees will be withheld at their proper time.

80.4 And the Moon will change its customary practice and will not appear at its proper time.

80.5 But in those days it will appear in Heaven, come on top of a large chariot in the west, and shine with more than normal brightness.

80.6 And many heads of the stars, in command, will go astray. And these will change their courses and their activities and will not appear at the times that have been prescribed for them.

80.7 And the entire law of the stars will be closed to the sinners, and the thoughts of those who dwell upon the Earth will go astray over them, and they will turn from all their ways and will go astray, and will think them gods.

80.8 And many evils will overtake them and punishment will come upon them to destroy them all."

81.1 And he said to me: "Oh Enoch, look at the book of the Tablets of Heaven and read what is written upon them, and note every individual fact."

81.2 And I looked at everything that was written and I noted everything. And I read the book and everything that was written in it, all the deeds of men, and all the children of flesh who will be upon the Earth, for all the generations of eternity.

81.3 And then I immediately blessed the Lord, the Eternal King of Glory, in that he has made all the works of the world, and I praised the Lord because of his patience, and I blessed him on account of the sons of Adam.

81.4 And at that time I said: "Blessed is the man who dies righteous and good, concerning whom no book of iniquity has been written, and against whom no guilt has been found."

81.5 And these three Holy ones brought me and set me on the earth in front of the door of my house, and said to me:

"Tell everything to your son Methuselah, and show all your children that no flesh is righteous, before the Lord, for He created them.

81.6 For one year we will leave you with your children, until you have regained your strength, so that you may teach your children and write these things down for them, and testify to all your children. And in the second year we will take you from amongst them.

81.7 Let your heart be strong, for the good will proclaim righteousness to the good, the righteous will rejoice with the righteous and they will wish each other well.

81.8 But the sinner will die with the sinner and the apostate will sink with the apostate.

81.9 And those who practice righteousness will die because of the deeds of men, and will be gathered in because of the deeds of the impious."

81.10 And in those days they finished speaking to me and I went to my family as I blessed the Lord of Ages.

82.1 And now, my son Methuselah,
all these things I recount to you, and write down for you. I have revealed everything to you, and have given you books about all these things. Keep, my son Methuselah, the books from the hand of your father so that you may pass them on to the generations of eternity.

82.2 I have given wisdom to you, and to your children, and to those who will be your children, that they may give it to their children, for all the generations, forever, this wisdom that is beyond their thoughts.

82.3 And those who understand it will not sleep, but will incline their ears that they may learn this wisdom, and it will be better for those who eat from it than good food.

82.4 Blessed are all the righteous, blessed are all those who walk in the way of righteousness and do not sin like the sinners. In the numbering of all their days in which the Sun journeys in Heaven, coming in and out, through the Gates of Heaven, for thirty days. With the leaders of the thousands, of this order of stars, and with the four which are added, and divided between the four seasons of the year, which lead them and appear with them on four days.

82.5 Because of them men go wrong, and they do not reckon them in the reckoning of the whole year; for men go wrong in respect of them and do not know them exactly.

82.6 For they belong in the reckoning of the year, and are truly recorded forever, one in the first Gate, and one in the third, and one in the fourth and one in the sixth. And the year is completed in 364 days.

82.7 And the account of it is true, and the recorded reckoning of it is exact, for the lights, and the months, and the feasts, and the years, and the days. Uriel showed me, and inspired me; he to whom the Lord of the whole created world gave commands about the Host of Heaven for me.

82.8 And he has power in Heaven, over night and day, to cause light to shine on men; the Sun, the Moon, and the stars, and all the Powers of Heaven, which rotate in their orbits.

82.9 And this is the Law of the Stars, which set in their places, at their times, and at their feasts, and in their months.

82.10 And these are the names of those who lead them, who keep watch, so that they appear at their times, and in their orders, and in their months, and in their periods of rule, and in their positions.

82.11 Their four leaders, who divide the four parts of the year, appear first; and after them the twelve leaders of the orders, who divide the months and the years into 364 days, with the heads over thousands, who separate the days. And for the four days, that are added to them, there are the leaders who separate the four parts of the year.

82.12 And as for these heads over thousands, one is added between the leader and the led, but their leaders make the separation.

82.13 And these are the names of the leaders who separate the four appointed parts of the year: Melkiel, Helemmelek, Meleyal, and Narel.

82.14 And the names of those whom they lead: Adnarel, Iyasusael, Iylumiel; these three follow behind the leaders of the orders. And all others follow behind the three leaders of the orders, who follow behind those leaders of positions, who separate the four parts of the year.

82.15 In the beginning of the year, Melkiel rises first and rules, who is called the southern Sun - and all the days of his period, during which he rules, are ninety-one.

82.16 And these are the signs of the days that are to be seen on the earth, in the days of his period of rule; sweat, and heat, and calm. And all the trees bear fruit, and leaves appear on all the trees, and the wheat harvest, and rose flowers. And all the flowers bloom in the field but the trees of winter are withered.

82.17 And these are the names of the leaders who are under them: Berkeel, Zelebsael, and another one who is added, a head over a thousand, named Heloyaseph. And the days of the period of rule, of this one, are complete.

82.18 The second leader, after him, is Helemmelec, whom they call the Shining Sun; and all the days of his light are ninety-one.

82.19 And these are the signs of the days on earth: heat, and drought. And the trees bring their fruit to ripeness and maturity and make their fruit dry. And the sheep mate and become pregnant. And men gather all the fruits of the earth, and everything that is in the fields, and the vats of wine. And these things occur in the days of his period of rule.

82.20 And these are the names, and the orders, and the leaders of these heads over thousands: Gedaeyal, Keel, and Heel. And the name of the head-over-athousand, who is added to them, is Asfael. And the days of his period of rule are complete.

SECTION IV.
CHAPTERS LXXXIII-XC.
THE DREAM-VISIONS.

83.1 And now, my son Methuselah, I will show you all the visions that I saw, recounting them before you.

83.2 Two visions I saw, before I took a wife, and neither one was like the other. For the first time, when I learnt the art of writing, and for the second time, before I took your mother. I saw a terrible vision and concerning this I made supplication to the Lord.

83.3 I had lain down in the house of my grandfather, Malalel, when I saw in a vision how Heaven was thrown down, and removed, and it fell upon the Earth.

83.4 And when it fell upon the Earth, I saw how the earth was swallowed up in a great abyss, and mountains were suspended on mountains, and hills sank down upon hills, and tall trees were torn up by their roots, and were thrown down, and sank into the abyss.

83.5 And then speech fell into my mouth, and I raised my voice to cry out, and said: "The earth is destroyed!"

83.6 And my grandfather, Malalel, roused me, since I lay near him, and said to me: "Why did you cry out so, my son, and why do you moan so?"

83.7 And I recounted to him the whole vision, which I had seen, and he said to me: "A terrible thing you have seen, my son! Your dream vision concerns the secrets of all the sin of the Earth; it is about to sink into the abyss and be utterly destroyed.

83.8 And now, my son, rise and make supplication to the Lord of Glory, for you are faithful, that a remnant may be left on the Earth and that he may not wipe out the whole Earth.

83.9 My son, from Heaven all this will come upon the Earth, and upon the Earth there will be great destruction."

83.10 And then I rose and prayed, and made supplication, and wrote my prayer down for the generations of eternity, and I will show everything to you my son Methuselah.

83.11 And, when I went out below and saw the sky, and the Sun rising in the east, and the Moon setting in the west, and some stars, and the whole Earth, and everything as He knew it since the beginning. Then I blessed the Lord of Judgment and ascribed Majesty to him, for he makes the Sun come out from the windows of the east, so that it ascends and rises on the face of Heaven, and follows the path which has been shown to it.

84.1 And I raised my hands in righteousness and I blessed the Holy and Great One. And I spoke with the breath of my mouth, and with the tongue of flesh, which God has made for men born of flesh so that they might speak with it; and he has given them breath, and a tongue, and a mouth, so that they might speak with them.

84.2 "Blessed are you, Oh Lord King, and great and powerful in your majesty, Lord of the whole Creation of Heaven, King of Kings, and God of the whole world! And your kingly authority, and your Sovereignty and your Majesty will last forever, and forever and ever, and your power, for all generations. And all the Heavens are your throne, forever, and the whole Earth your footstool forever, and ever and ever.

84.3 For you made, and you rule, everything, and nothing is too hard for you, and no wisdom escapes you; it does not turn away from your throne nor from your presence. And you know, and see, and hear, everything, and nothing is hidden from you, for you see everything.

84.4 And now the Angels of your Heaven are doing wrong and your anger rests upon the flesh of men until the day of the great judgment.

84.5 And now, Oh God, Lord, and Great King, I entreat and ask that you will fulfill my prayer to leave me a posterity on Earth and not to wipe out all the flesh of men and make the earth empty so that there is destruction forever.

84.6 And now, my Lord, wipe out from the earth the flesh that has provoked your anger, but the flesh of righteousness and uprightness establish as a seed-bearing plant forever. And do not hide your face from the prayer of your servant, Oh Lord."

85.1 And after this I saw another dream, and I will show it all to you, my son.

85.2 And Enoch raised his voice and said to his son Methuselah: "To you I speak, my son. Hear my words, and incline your ear to the dream vision of your father.

85.3 Before I took your mother, Edna, I saw a vision on my bed: - and behold - a bull came out of the earth, and that bull was white.

And, after it, a heifer came out, and with the heifer came two bullocks, and one of them was black and the other red.

85.4 And that black bullock struck the red one, and pursued it over the earth, and from then on I could not see that red bullock.

85.5 But that black bullock grew, and a heifer went with it; and I saw that many bulls came out from it, which were like it, and followed behind it.

85.6 And that cow, that first one, came from the presence of that first bull, seeking that red bullock, but did not find it. And then it moaned bitterly and continued to seek it.

85.7 And I looked until that first bull came to it, and calmed it, and from that time it did not cry out.

85.8 And after this, she bore another white bull, and after this she bore many black bulls and cows.

85.9 And I saw, in my sleep, that white bull, how it likewise grew and became a large white bull. And from it came many white bulls, and they were like it.

85.10 And they began to beget many white bulls that were like them - one following another.

86.1 And again, I looked with my eyes as I was sleeping, and I saw Heaven above, and behold, a star fell from Heaven, and it arose and ate and pastured amongst those bulls.

86.2 And, after this, I saw the large and the black bulls, and behold, all of them changed their pens, and their pastures, and their heifers. And they began to moan, one after another.

86.3 And, again, I saw in the vision and looked up at Heaven, and behold, I saw many stars, how they came down, and were thrown down from Heaven to that first star, and fell amongst those heifers and bulls. They were with them pasturing amongst them.

86.4 And I looked at them and saw, and behold, all of them let out their private parts, like horses, and began to mount the cows of the bulls. And they all became pregnant and bore elephants, camels, and asses.

86.5 And all the bulls were afraid of them, and were terrified in front of them. And they began to bite with their teeth, and to devour, and to gore with their horns.

86.6 And so they began to devour those bulls, and behold, all the sons of the Earth began to tremble and shake before them and to flee.

87.1 And again I saw them, how they began to gore one another, and to devour one another, and the Earth began to cry out.

87.2 And I raised my eyes again to Heaven, and saw in the vision, and behold, there came from Heaven beings that were like white men. And four came from that place, and three others with them.

87.3 And those three, who came out last, took hold of me by my hand and raised me from the generations of the Earth, and lifted me up onto a high place, and showed me a tower high above the earth, and all the hills were lower.

87.4 And one said to me: "Remain here until you have seen everything which is coming upon these elephants, and camels, and asses, and upon the stars, and upon all the bulls."

88.1 And I saw one of those four who had come out first, how he took hold of that first star, which had fallen from Heaven, and bound it by its hands and feet, and threw it into an abyss. And that abyss was narrow, and deep, and horrible, and dark.

88.2 And one of them drew his sword, and gave it to those elephants, camels, and asses; and they began to strike one another, and the whole Earth shook because of them.

88.3 And as I looked in the vision, behold, one of those four who had come out cast a line from Heaven and gathered and took all the large stars; those whose private parts were like the private parts of horses, and bound them all by their hands and their feet, and threw them into a chasm of the Earth.

89.1 And one of those four, went to a white bull, and taught him a mystery, trembling as he was. He was born a bull, but became a man, and built for himself a large vessel, and dwelt on it, and three bulls went with him in that vessel, and they were covered over.

89.2 And, again, I raised my eyes to Heaven and saw a high roof with seven water channels on it, and those channels discharged much water into an enclosure.

89.3 And I looked again, and behold, springs opened on the floor of that large enclosure, and water began to bubble up, and to rise above the floor. And I looked at that enclosure until its whole floor was covered by water.

89.4 And water, darkness, and mist increased on it, and I looked at the height of that water, and that water had risen above that enclosure and was pouring out over the enclosure, and it remained on the earth.

89.5 And all the bulls of that enclosure were gathered together, until I saw how they sank, and were swallowed up, and destroyed, in that water.

89.6 And that vessel floated on the water, but all the bulls, elephants, camels, and asses sank to the bottom, together with all the animals, so that I could not see them. And they were unable to get out, but were destroyed, and sank into the depths.

89.7 And, again, I looked at that vision until those water channels were removed from that high roof, and the chasms of the Earth were made level, and other abysses were opened.

89.8 And the water began to run down into them, until the earth became visible, and that vessel settled on the earth and the darkness departed, and light appeared.

89.9 And that white bull, who became a man, went out from that vessel, and the three bulls with him. And one of the three bulls was white, like that bull, and one of them was red as blood, and one was black. And that white bull passed away from them.

89.10 And they began to beget wild animals and birds, so that there arose from them every kind of species: lions, tigers, wolves, dogs, hyenas, wildboars, foxes, badgers, pigs, falcons, vultures, kites, eagles, and ravens. But amongst them was born a white bull.

89.11 And they began to bite one another but that white bull, which was born amongst them, begat a wild ass and a white bull with it, and the wild asses increased.

89.12 But that bull, which was born from it, begat a black wild boar and a white sheep, and that wild-boar begat many boars and that sheep begat twelve sheep.

89.13 And when those twelve sheep had grown, they handed one of their number over to the asses, and those in turn, handed that sheep over to the wolves; and that sheep grew up amongst the wolves.

89.14 And the Lord brought the eleven sheep to dwell with it, and to pasture with it amongst the wolves, and they increased and became many flocks of sheep.

89.15 And the wolves began to make them afraid, and they oppressed them until they made away with their young, and then they threw their young into a river with much water; but those sheep began to cry out because of their young, and to complain to their Lord.

89.16 But a sheep, which had been saved from the wolves, fled and escaped to the wild asses. And I saw the sheep moaning and crying out, and petitioning the Lord with all their power, until that Lord of the sheep came down at the call of the sheep, from a high room, and came to them, and looked at them.

89.17 And he called that sheep, which had fled from the wolves, and spoke to it about the wolves, that it should warn them that they should not touch the sheep.

89.18 And the sheep went to the wolves, in accordance with the Word of the Lord, and another sheep met that sheep and went with it. And the two of them together, entered the assembly of those wolves, spoke to them, and warned them that from then on, they should not touch those sheep.

89.19 And after this, I saw the wolves, how they acted even more harshly towards the sheep, with all their power, and the sheep called out.

89.20 And their Lord came to the sheep and began to beat those wolves; and the wolves began to moan, but the sheep became silent and from then on they did not cry out.

89.21 And I looked at the sheep until they escaped from the wolves; but the eyes of the wolves were blinded, and those wolves went out in pursuit of the sheep with all their forces.

89.22 And the Lord of the sheep went with them, as he led them, and all his sheep followed him; and his face was glorious, and his appearance terrible and magnificent.

89.23 But the wolves began to pursue those sheep until they met them by a stretch of water.

89.24 And that stretch of water was divided, and the water stood on one side, and on the other, before them. And their Lord as he led them, stood between them and the wolves.

89.25 And while those wolves had not yet seen the sheep, they went into the middle of that stretch of water; but the wolves pursued the sheep, and those wolves ran after them into that stretch of water.

89.26 But when they saw the Lord of the sheep they turned to flee in front of him; but that stretch of water flowed together again, and suddenly resumed its natural form, and the water swelled up, and rose until it covered those wolves.

89.27 And I looked until all the wolves that had pursued those sheep were destroyed and drowned.

89.28 But the sheep escaped that water, and went to a desert, where there was neither water, nor grass. And they began to open their eyes and see, and I saw the Lord of the sheep pasturing them, and giving them water and grass, and that sheep going and leading them.

89.29 And that sheep went up to the summit of a high rock and the Lord of the sheep sent it to them.

89.30 And after this, I saw the Lord of the sheep standing before them, and his appearance was terrible and majestic, and all those sheep saw him and were afraid of him.

89.31 And all of them were afraid and trembled before him; and they cried out to that sheep, with those who were in their midst: "We cannot stand before our Lord nor look at him."

89.32 And that sheep, which led them, again went up to the summit of that rock; and the sheep began to be blinded, and go astray from the path which had been shown to them, but that sheep did not know.

89.33 And the Lord of the sheep was extremely angry with them, and that sheep knew, and went down from the summit of the rock, and came to the sheep, and found the majority of them, with their eyes blinded, and going astray from his path.

89.34 And when they saw it they were afraid and trembled before it and wished that they could return to their enclosure. And that sheep took some other sheep with it, and went to those sheep that had gone astray, and then began to kill them; and the sheep were afraid of it. And that sheep brought back those sheep that had gone astray, and they returned to their enclosures.

89.36 And I looked there at the vision, until that sheep became a man, and built a house for the Lord of the sheep, and made all the sheep stand in that house.

89.37 And I looked until that sheep, which had met that sheep that led the sheep, fell asleep. And I looked until all the large sheep were destroyed and small ones arose in their place, and they came to a pasture, and drew near a river of water.

89.38 And that sheep that led them, which had become a man, separated from them and fell asleep, and all the sheep sought it, and cried out very bitterly over it.

89.39 And I looked until they left off crying for that sheep, and crossed that river of water. And there arose all the sheep that led them, in place of those which had fallen asleep; and they led.

89.40 And I looked until the sheep came to a good place and a pleasant and glorious land, and I looked until those sheep were satisfied. And that house was in the middle of them in that green and pleasant land.

89.41 And sometimes their eyes were opened, and sometimes blinded, until another sheep rose up, led them, and brought them all back. And their eyes were opened.

89.42 And the dogs, and the foxes, and the wild boars, began to devour those sheep until the Lord of the sheep raised up a ram from among them, which led them.

89.43 And that ram began to butt those dogs, foxes, and wild boars, on one side and on the other until it had destroyed them all.

89.44 And the eyes of that sheep were opened, and it saw that ram in the middle of the sheep, how it renounced its glory, and began to butt those sheep, and how it trampled on them and behaved unbecomingly.

89.45 And the Lord of the sheep sent the sheep to another sheep and raised it up to be a ram and to lead the sheep in place of that sheep which had renounced its glory.

89.46 And it went to it, and spoke with it alone, and raised up that ram, and made it the prince and leader of the sheep. And, during all this, those dogs oppressed the sheep.

89.47 And the first ram pursued that second ram and that second ram rose and fled before it. And I looked until those dogs made the first ram fall.

89.48 And that second ram rose up and led the small sheep, and that ram begat many sheep, and fell asleep. And a small sheep became a ram, in place of it, and became the prince and leader of those sheep.

89.49 And those sheep grew and increased; but all the dogs, and foxes, and wild boars, were afraid and fled from it. And that ram butted and killed all the animals, and those animals did not again prevail amongst the sheep, and did not seize anything further from them.

89.50 And that house became large and broad, and for those sheep a high tower was built on that house for the Lord of the sheep. And that house was low but the tower was raised up and high. And the Lord of the sheep stood on that tower and they spread a full table before him.

89.51 And I saw those sheep again, how they went astray, and walked in many ways, and left that house of theirs; and the Lord of the sheep called some of the sheep, and sent them to the sheep, but the sheep began to kill them.

89.52 But one of them was saved, and was not killed, and it sprang away and cried out against the sheep. And they wished to kill it but the Lord of the sheep saved it from the hands of the sheep, brought it up to me, and made it stay.

89.53 And he sent many other sheep to those sheep, to testify to them and to lament over them.

89.54 And after this, I saw how when they left the house of the Lord of the sheep, and his tower, they went astray in everything, and their eyes were blinded. And I saw how the Lord of the sheep wrought much slaughter among them, in their pastures, until those sheep invited that slaughter, and betrayed his place.

89.55 And he gave them into the hands of the lions, and the tigers, and the wolves, and the hyenas, and into the hands of the foxes, and to all the animals. And those wild animals began to tear those sheep in pieces.

89.56 And I saw how he left that house of theirs, and their tower, and gave them all into the hands of the lions so that they might tear them in pieces and devour them, and into the hands of all the animals.

89.57 And I began to cry out with all my power, to call the Lord of the sheep, and to represent to him concerning the sheep; that all the wild animals were devouring them.

89.58 But he remained still, although he saw, and he rejoiced that they were devoured, swallowed up and carried off. And he gave them into the hands of all the animals for food.

89.59 And he called seventy shepherds, and cast off those sheep, so that they might pasture them. And he said to the shepherds and to their companions: "Each one of you, from now on, is to pasture the sheep and do whatever I command you.

89.60 And I will hand them over to you, duly numbered, and I will tell you which of them are to be destroyed, and destroy them." And he handed those sheep over to them.

89.61 And he called another, and said to him: "Observe and see everything that these shepherds do against these sheep for they will destroy from among them more than I have commanded them.

89.62 And write down all the excess and destruction, which is wrought by the shepherds; how many they destroy at my command and how many they destroy of their own volition. Write down against each shepherd, individually, all that he destroys.

89.63 And read out in front of me exactly how many they destroy of their own volition and how many are handed over for destruction so that this may be a testimony for me against them. So that I may know all the deeds of the shepherds in order to hand them over for judgment. And I will see what they do, whether they abide by my command with which I have commanded them, or not.

89.64 But they must not know this, and you must not show this to them, but only write down against each individual in his time all that the shepherds destroy, and bring it all up to me."

89.65 And I looked until those shepherds pastured at their times, and they began to kill and destroy more than they were commanded, and they gave those sheep into the hands of the lions. **89.66** And the lions and the tigers devoured and swallowed up the majority of those sheep, and the wild boars devoured with them; and they burnt down that tower and demolished that house.

89.67 And I was extremely sad about that tower because that house of the sheep had been demolished; and after that I was unable to see whether those sheep went into that house.

89.68 And the shepherds and their companions handed those sheep over to all the animals so that they might devour them. Each one of them, at his time, received an exact number, and for each of them, one after the other, there was written in a book how many of them were destroyed.

89.69 And each one killed and destroyed more than was prescribed and I began to weep and moan very much because of those sheep.

89.70 And likewise, in the vision, I saw that one who wrote, how each day, he wrote down each one that was destroyed by those shepherds. And he brought up, and presented, the whole book to the Lord of the sheep, everything they had done and all that each one of them had made away with, and all that they had handed to destruction.

89.71 And the book was read out in front of the Lord of the sheep, and he took the book in his hand, read it, sealed it, and put it down.

89.72 And after this I saw how the shepherds pastured for twelve hours, and behold three of those sheep returned, and arrived, and came and began to build up all that had fallen down from that house; but the wild boars hindered them so that they could not.

89.73 And they again began to build, as before, and they raised up that tower, and it was called the high tower. And they began again to place a table before the tower but all the bread on it was unclean and was not pure.

89.74 And, besides all this, the eyes of these sheep were blinded so that they could not see, and their shepherds likewise. And they handed yet more of them over to destruction, and they trampled on the sheep with their feet, and devoured them.

89.75 But the Lord of the sheep remained still, until all the sheep were scattered abroad, and had mixed with them, and they did not save them from the hands of the animals.

89.76 And that one who wrote the book brought it up, showed it, and read it out in the dwelling of the Lord of the sheep. And he entreated Him on behalf of them, and petitioned Him, as he showed Him all the deeds of their shepherds and testified in front of Him against all the shepherds.

89.77 And he took the book, put it down by Him, and went out.

90.1 And I looked until the time that thirty-five shepherds had pastured the sheep the same way, and, each individually; they all completed their time like the first ones. And others received them into their hands to pasture them, at their time, each shepherd at his own time.

90.2 And after this, I saw in the vision, all the birds of the sky coming: - The eagles, the vultures, and the kites, and the ravens. But the eagles led all the birds, and they began to devour those sheep, to peck out their eyes, and to devour their flesh.

90.3 And the sheep cried out because the birds devoured their flesh. And I cried out and lamented in my sleep because of that shepherd who pastured the sheep.

90.4 And I looked until those sheep were devoured by those dogs, and by the eagles, and by the kites, and they left them neither flesh nor skin, nor sinew, until only their bones remained. And their bones fell upon the ground and the sheep became few.

90.5 And I looked until the time that twenty-three shepherds had pastured, and they completed, each in his time, fifty eight times.

90.6 And small lambs were born from those white sheep, and they began to open their eyes, to see, and to cry to the sheep.

90.7 But the sheep did not cry to them, and did not listen to what they said to them, but were extremely deaf, and their eyes were extremely and excessively blinded.

90.8 And I saw in the vision, how the ravens flew upon those lambs, and took one of those lambs, and dashed the sheep in pieces and devoured them.

90.9 And I looked until horns came up on those lambs but the ravens cast their horns down. And I looked until a big horn grew on one of those sheep, and their eyes were opened.

90.10 And it looked at them and their eyes were opened. And it cried to the sheep, and the rams saw it, and they all ran to it.

90.11 And, besides all this, those eagles, and vultures, and ravens, and kites, were still continually tearing the sheep in pieces, and flying upon them and devouring them. And the sheep were silent but the rams lamented and cried out.

90.12 And those ravens battled and fought with it, and wished to make away with its horn, but they did not prevail against it.

90.13 And I looked at them until the shepherds and the eagles, and those vultures, and kites, came and cried to the ravens that they should dash the horn of that ram in pieces. And they fought and battled with it, and it fought with them and cried out so that its help might come to it.

90.14 And I looked until that man, who wrote down the names of the shepherds and brought them up before the Lord of the sheep, came, and he helped that ram and showed it everything; its help was coming down.

90.15 And I looked until that Lord of the sheep came to them in anger, all those who saw him fled, and they all fell into the shadow in front of Him.

90.16 All the eagles and vultures and ravens and kites, gathered together and brought with them all the wild sheep, and they all came together and helped one another in order to dash that horn of the ram in pieces.

90.17 And I looked at that man, who wrote the book at the command of the Lord, until he opened that book of the destruction that those last twelve shepherds had wrought. And he showed, in front of the Lord of the sheep, that they had destroyed even more than those before them had.

90.18 And I looked until the Lord of the sheep came to them and took the Staff of His Anger and struck the Earth. And the Earth was split. And all the animals, and the birds of the sky, fell from those sheep and sank in the earth; and it closed over them.

90.19 And I looked until a big sword was given to the sheep. And the sheep went out against all the wild animals to kill them. And all the animals, and birds of the sky, fled before them.

90.20 And I looked until a throne was set up in a pleasant land and the Lord of the sheep sat on it. And they took all the sealed books and opened the books in front of the Lord of the sheep.

90.21 And the Lord called those men, the seven first white ones, and commanded them to bring in front of Him the first star, which went before those stars whose private parts were like horses, and they brought them all in front of Him.

90.22 And He said to that man who wrote in front of Him, who was one of the seven white ones, He said to him: "Take those seventy shepherds, to whom I handed over the sheep, and who, on their own authority, took and killed more than I commanded them."

90.23 And behold, I saw them all bound, and they all stood in front of Him.

90.24 And the judgment was held, first on the stars, and they were judged and found guilty, and they went to the place of damnation, and were thrown into a deep place full of fire burning, and full of pillars of fire.

90.25 And those seventy shepherds were judged, and found guilty, and they also were thrown into that abyss of fire.

90.26 And I saw at that time, how a similar abyss was opened in the middle of the Earth which was full of fire, and they brought those blind sheep and they were all judged, and found guilty, and thrown into that abyss of fire and they burned. And that abyss was on the south of that house.

90.27 And I saw those sheep burning and their bones were burning.

90.28 And I stood up to look until he folded up that old house, and they removed all the pillars, and all the beams and ornaments of that house were folded up with it. And they removed it and put it in a place in the south of the land.

90.29 And I looked until the Lord of the sheep brought a new house, larger and higher than the first one, and he set it up on the site of the first one that had been folded up. And all its pillars were new, and its ornaments were new and larger than those of the first one - the old one that had been removed. And the Lord of the sheep was in the middle of it.

90.30 And I saw all the sheep that were left, and all the animals of the earth, and all the birds of the sky, falling down and worshipping those sheep, and entreating them and obeying them in every command.

90.31 And after this, those three who were dressed in white and had taken hold of my hand, the ones who had brought me up at first. They, with the hand of that ram also holding me, took me up, and put me down in the middle of those sheep before the judgment was held.

90.32 And those sheep were all white and their wool thick and pure.

90.33 And all those which had been destroyed and scattered, and all the wild animals, and all the birds of the sky, gathered together in that house, and the Lord of the sheep rejoiced

THE BOOKS OF ENOCH

very much because they were all good, and had returned to His house.

90.34 And I looked until they had laid down that sword, which had been given to the sheep, and they brought it back into his house, and it was sealed in front of the Lord. And all the sheep were enclosed in that house but it did not hold them.

90.35 And the eyes of all of them were opened, and they saw well, and there was not one among them that did not see.

90.36 And I saw that that house was large, broad, and exceptionally full.

90.37 And I saw how a white bull was born, and its horns were big, and all the wild animals, and all the birds of the sky, were afraid of it, and entreated it continually.

90.38 And I looked until all their species were transformed and they all became white bulls. And the first among them was a wild-ox. And that wild-ox was a large animal and had big black horns on its head. And the Lord of the sheep rejoiced over them, and over all the bulls.

90.39 And I was asleep in the middle of them and I woke up and saw everything.

90.40 And this is the vision which I saw while I was asleep, and I woke up, blessed the Lord of Righteousness, and ascribed glory to him.

90.41 But after this I wept bitterly and my tears did not stop until I could not endure it. When I looked, they ran down, because of what I saw, for everything will come to pass and be fulfilled, and all the deeds of men, in their order, were shown to me.

90.42 That night I remembered my first dream, and because of it I wept, and was disturbed, because I had seen that vision.

SECTION V.
CHAPTERS XCI-CIV
A BOOK OF EXHORTATION AND PROMISED BLESSING FOR THE RIGHTEOUS AND OF MALEDICTION AND WOE FOR THE SINNERS.

91.1 And now my son Methuselah, call to me all your brothers, and gather to me all the children of your mother. For a voice calls me, and a spirit has been poured over me, so that I may show you everything that will come upon you forever.

91.2 And after this Methuselah went and called his brothers to him and gathered his relations.

91.3 And he spoke about righteousness to all his sons, and said: "Hear, my children, all the words of your father, and listen properly to the voice of my mouth, for I will testify and speak to you - my beloved. Love uprightness and walk in it!

91.4 And do not draw near to uprightness with a double heart, and do not associate with those of a double heart, but walk in righteousness my children and it will lead you in good paths, and righteousness will be your companion.

91.5 For I know that the state of wrongdoing will continue on Earth, and a great punishment will be carried out on the Earth, and an end will be made of all iniquity. And it will be cut off at its roots and its whole edifice will pass away.

91.6 And iniquity will again be complete on the Earth, and all the deeds of iniquity, and the deeds of wrong, and of wickedness, will prevail for a second time."

91.7 And when iniquity, and sin, and blasphemy, and wrong, and all kinds of evil deeds increase, and when apostasy, wickedness, and uncleanness increase, a great punishment will come from Heaven upon all these. And the Holy Lord will come in anger, and in wrath, to execute judgment on the Earth.

91.8 In those days wrongdoing will be cut off at its roots, and the roots of iniquity, together with deceit, will be destroyed from under Heaven.

91.9 And all the idols of the nations will be given up, their towers will be burnt in fire, and they will remove them from the whole Earth. And they will be thrown down into the Judgment of Fire, and will be destroyed in anger, and in the severe judgment that is forever.

91.10 And the righteous will rise from sleep, and wisdom will rise, and will be given to them.

91.11 And after this the roots of iniquity will be cut off and the sword will destroy the sinners. The blasphemers will be cut off; in every place blasphemy will be destroyed by the sword.

91.12 And after this there will be another week; **the eighth**, that of righteousness, and a sword will be given to it so that the Righteous Judgment may be executed on those who do wrong, and the sinners will be handed over into the hands of the righteous.

91.13 And, at its end, they will acquire Houses because of their righteousness, and a House will be built for the Great King in Glory, forever.

91.14 And after this, in the **ninth week**, the Righteous Judgment will be revealed to the whole world. And all the deeds of the impious will vanish from the whole Earth. And the world will be written down for destruction and all men will look to the Path of Uprightness.

91.15 And, after this, in the **tenth week**, in the seventh part, there will be an Eternal Judgment that will be executed on the Watchers and the Great Eternal Heaven that will spring from the midst of the Angels.

91.16 And the First Heaven will vanish and pass away and a New Heaven will appear, and all the Powers of Heaven will shine forever, with sevenfold light.

91.17 And after this, there will be many weeks without number, forever, in goodness and in righteousness. And from then on sin will never again be mentioned.

91.18 And now I tell you, my children, and show you the paths of righteousness, and the paths of wrongdoing. And I will show you again so that you may know what is to come.

91.19 And now listen, my children, walk in the paths of righteousness and do not walk in the paths of wrongdoing, for all those who walk in the path of iniquity will be destroyed forever.

92.1 Written by Enoch-the-Scribe, this complete wisdom and teaching, praised by all men and a judge of the whole Earth. For all my sons who dwell on Earth. And for the last generations who will practice justice and peace.

92.2 Let not your spirit be saddened by the times for the Holy and Great One has appointed days for all things.

92.3 And the righteous man will rise from sleep, will rise and will walk in the path of righteousness, and all his paths, and his journeys, will be in eternal goodness and mercy.

92.4 He will show mercy to the righteous man and to him give eternal uprightness, and to him give power. And he will live in goodness, and righteousness, and will walk in eternal light.

92.5 And sin will be destroyed in darkness, forever, and from that day will never again be seen.

93.1 And, after this, Enoch began to speak from the books:

93.2 And Enoch said: "Concerning the sons of righteousness, and concerning the chosen of the world, and concerning the plant of righteousness and uprightness, I will speak these things to you, and make them known to you, my children.

I, Enoch, according to that which appeared to me in the Heavenly vision, and that which I know from the words of the Holy Angels, and understanding from the Tablets of Heaven."

93.3 And Enoch then began to speak from the books, and said: "I was born the seventh, in the **first week**, while justice and righteousness still lasted.

93.4 And, after me, in the **second week**, great injustice will arise, and

deceit will have sprung up. And in it there will be the First End, and in it, a man will be saved. And after it has ended, iniquity will grow, and He will make a law for the sinners.

93.5 And after this in the **third week**, at its end, a man will be chosen as the Plant of Righteous Judgment, and after him will come the Plant of Righteousness, forever.

93.6 And after this, in the **fourth week**, at its end, visions of the righteous and Holy will be seen, and a Law for All Generations, and an enclosure will be made for them.

93.7 And after this, in the **fifth week**, at its end, a House of Glory and Sovereignty will be built forever.

93.8 And after this, in the **sixth week**, all those who live in it will be blinded. And the hearts of them all, lacking wisdom, will sink into impiety. And in it, a man will ascend, and at its end the House of Sovereignty will be burnt with fire. And in it the whole race of the chosen root will be scattered.

93.9 And after this, in the **seventh week**, an apostate generation will arise. And many will be its deeds - but all its deeds will be apostasy.

93.10 And at its end, the Chosen Righteous, from the Eternal Plant of Righteousness, will be chosen, to whom will be given sevenfold teaching, concerning his whole creation.

93.11 For is there any man who can hear the voice of the Holy One and not be disturbed? And who is there who can think his thoughts? And who is there who can look at all the works of Heaven?

93.12 And how should there be anyone who could understand the works of Heaven, and see a soul, or a spirit, and tell about it, or ascend and see all their ends and comprehend them, or make anything like them?

93.13 And is there any man who could know the length and breadth of the Earth? And to who has all its measurements been shown?

93.14 Or is there any man who could know the length of Heaven, and what is its height, and on what is it fixed, and how large is the number of stars, and where do all the lights rest?

94.1 And now I say to you, my children, love righteousness and walk in it; for the paths of righteousness are worthy of acceptance, but the paths of iniquity will quickly be destroyed and vanish.

94.2 And to certain men, from a future generation, the paths of wrongdoing and of death will be revealed; and they will keep away from them and will not follow them.

94.3 And now I say to you, the righteous: do not walk in the wicked path, or in wrongdoing, or in the paths of death, and do not draw near to them or you may be destroyed.

94.4 But seek, and choose for yourself, righteousness, and a life that is pleasing and walk in the paths of peace so that you may live and prosper.

94.5 And hold my words firmly in the thoughts of your heart, and do not let them be erased from your heart, for I know that sinners will tempt men to debase wisdom, and no place will be found for it, and temptation will in no way decrease.

94.6 Woe to those who build iniquity and found deceit for they will quickly be thrown down and will not have peace.

94.7 Woe to those who build their houses with sin, for from their whole foundation they will be thrown down, and by the sword they shall fall, and those who acquire gold and silver will quickly be destroyed in the judgment.

94.8 Woe to you, you rich, for you have trusted in your riches, but from your riches you will depart for you did not remember the Most High in the days of your riches.

94.9 You have committed blasphemy, and iniquity, and are ready for the days of the outpouring of blood, and for the day of darkness, and for the day of the Great Judgment.

94.10 Thus I say, and make known to you, that He who created you will throw you down, and over your fall there will be no mercy, but your creator will rejoice at your destruction.

94.11 And your righteousness in those days will be a reproach to the sinners and to the impious.

95.1 Would that my eyes were a raincloud, so that I might weep over you, and pour out my tears like rain, so that I might have rest from the sorrow of my heart!

95.2 Who permitted you to practice hatred and wickedness? May judgment come upon you, the sinners!

95.3 Do not be afraid of the sinners, you righteous, for the Lord will again deliver them into your hands, so that you may execute judgment on them as you desire.

95.4 Woe to you who pronounce anathema that you cannot remove. Healing will be far from you because of your sin.

95.5 Woe to you who repay your neighbours with evil for you will be repaid according to your deeds.

95.6 Woe to you, you lying witnesses, and to those who weigh out iniquity, for you will quickly be destroyed.

95.7 Woe to you, you sinners, because you persecute the righteous, for you yourselves will be handed over and persecuted, you men of iniquity, and their yoke will be heavy on you.

96.1 Be hopeful, you righteous, for the sinners will quickly be destroyed before you, and you will have power over them, as you desire.

96.2 And in the day of the distress of the sinners, your young will rise up, like eagles, and your nest will be higher than that of vultures. And you will go up, and like badgers, enter the crevices of the earth, and the clefts of the rock, forever, before the lawless, but they will groan and weep because of you, like satyrs.

96.3 And do not be afraid you who have suffered, for you will receive healing, and a bright light will shine upon you, and the Voice of Rest you will hear from Heaven.

96.4 Woes to you, you sinners, for your riches make you appear righteous, but your hearts prove you to be sinners. And this word will be a testimony against you as a reminder of your evil deeds.

96.5 Woe to you who devour the finest of the wheat, and drink the best of the water, and trample upon the humble through your power.

96.6 Woe to you who drink water all the time, for you will quickly be repaid, and will become exhausted and dry for you have left the spring of life.

96.7 Woe to you who commit iniquity, and deceit, and blasphemy, it will be a reminder of evil against you.

96.8 Woe to you, you powerful, who through power oppress the righteous; for the day of your destruction will come.

In those days many good days will come for the righteous in the day of your judgment.

97.1 Believe, you righteous, that the sinners will become an object of shame and will be destroyed on the Day of Judgment.

97.2 Be it known to you, sinners, that the Most High remembers your destruction and that the Angels rejoice over your destruction.

97.3 What will you do, you sinners, and where will you flee on that day of judgment when you hear the sound of prayer of the righteous?

97.4 But you will not be like them against whom this word will be a testimony:

"You have been associated with the sinners."

97.5 And in those days, the prayer of the Holy will be in front of the Lord, and for you will come the days of your judgment.

97.6 And the words of your iniquity will be read out before the Great and Holy One, and your faces will blush with shame, and every deed which is founded upon iniquity will be rejected.

97.7 Woe to you, you sinners, who are in the middle of the sea, or on dry ground, their memory will be harmful to you.

97.8 Woe to you who acquire silver and gold, but not in righteousness, and say: "We have become very rich and have possessions, and have acquired everything that we desired.

97.9 And now let us do what we planned, for we have gathered silver and filled our storehouses, and as many as water are the servants of our houses."

97.10 And like the water your life will flow away, for your riches will not stay with you, but will quickly go up from you, for you acquired everything in iniquity and you will be given over to a great curse.

98.1 Now I swear to you, the wise, and the foolish, that you will see many things on the earth.

98.2 For you men will put on yourselves more adornments than a woman, and more coloured garments than a girl, clothed in sovereignty, and in majesty, and in power, and silver, and gold, and purple, and honours, - and food will be poured out like water.

98.3 Because of this they will have neither knowledge nor wisdom. And through this, they will be destroyed, together with their possessions, and with all their glory and their honour. And in shame, and in slaughter, and in great destitution, their spirits will be thrown into the fiery furnace.

98.4 I swear to you, you sinners, that as a mountain has not, and will not, become a slave, nor a hill a woman's maid, so sin was not sent on the Earth but man, of himself, created it. And those who commit it will be subject to a great curse.

98.5 And barrenness has not been given to a woman but because of the deeds of her hand she dies without children.

98.6 I swear to you, you sinners, by the Holy and Great One, that all your evil deeds are revealed in Heaven and that your wrongdoing is not covered or hidden.

98.7 And do not think in your spirit nor say in your heart, that you do not know, or do not see, every sin is written down every day in Heaven in front of the Most High.

98.8 From now on, you know that all your wrongdoing that you do will be written down every day, until the day of your judgment.

98.9 Woe to you, you fools, for you will be destroyed through your folly. And you do not listen to the wise and good will not come upon you.

98.10 And now know that you are ready for the day of destruction. And do not hope that you will live, you sinners; rather you will go and die, for you know no ransom. You are ready for the Day of the Great Judgment and for the day of distress and great shame for your spirits.

98.11 Woe to you, you stubborn of heart who do evil and eat blood, from where do you have good things to eat and drink and to be satisfied? From all the good things which our Lord the Most High has placed in abundance on the earth. Therefore you will not have peace.

98.12 Woe to you who love deeds of iniquity. Why do you hope for good for yourselves? Know that you will be given into the hands of the righteous, and they will cut your throats and kill you, and will not have mercy on you.

98.13 Woe to you who rejoice in the distress of the righteous for graves will not be dug for you.

98.14 Woe to you who declare the words of the righteous empty for you will have no hope of life.

98.15 Woe to you who write lying words, and the words of the impious, for they write their lies so that men may hear and continue their folly. And they will not have peace but will die a sudden death.

99

.1 Woe to you who do impious deeds and praise and honour lying words; you will be destroyed and will not have a good life.

99.2 Woe to you who alter the words of truth, and they distort the eternal law and count themselves as being without sin; they will be trampled underfoot on the ground.

99.3 In those days make ready, you righteous, to raise your prayers as a reminder and lay them as a testimony before the Angels, that they may lay the sin of the sinners before the Most High as a reminder.

99.4 In those days the nations will be thrown into confusion and the races of the nations will rise on the Day of Destruction.

99.5 And in those days, those who are in need will go out, seize their children, and cast out their children. And their offspring will slip from them, and they will cast out their children while they are still sucklings, and will not return to them, and will not have mercy on their beloved ones.

99.6 And again I swear to you, the sinners, that sin is ready for the Day of Unceasing Bloodshed.

99.7 And they worship stone, and some carve images of gold and of silver, and of wood and of clay. And some, with no knowledge, worship unclean spirits and demons, and every kind of error. But no help will be obtained from them.

99.8 And they will sink into impiety because of the folly of their hearts, and their eyes will be blinded through the fear of their hearts, and through the vision of their ambitions.

99.9 Through these they will become impious and fearful, for they do all their deeds with lies, and worship stones, and they will be destroyed at the same moment.

99.10 And in those days, blessed are those who accept the words of wisdom, and understand them, and follow the paths of the Most High, and walk in the path of righteousness, and do not act impiously with the impious, for they will be saved.

99.11 Woe to you who extend evil to your neighbours; for you will be killed in Sheol.

99.12 Woe to you who lay foundations of sin and deceit, and who cause bitterness on the Earth, for because of this an end will be made of them.

99.13 Woe to you who build your houses with the toil of others, and all their building materials are the sticks and stones of sin; I say to you: "You will not have peace."

99.14 Woe to those who reject the measure, and the eternal inheritance of their fathers, and cause their souls to follow error, for they will not have rest.

99.15 Woe to those who commit iniquity, and help wrong, and kill their neighbours, until the Day of the Great Judgment; for he will throw down your glory.

99.16 And you put evil into your hearts, and rouse the spirit of his anger, so that he may destroy you all with the sword. And all the righteous and the Holy will remember your sin.

100.1 And in those days, and in one place, fathers and sons will strike one another, and brothers will together fall in death, until their blood flows as if it were a stream.

100.2 For a man will not, in mercy, withhold his hand from his sons, nor from his son's sons, in order to kill them. And the sinner will not withhold his hand from his honoured brother from dawn until the Sun sets they will kill one another.

100.3 And the horse will walk up to its chest in the blood of sinners and the chariot will sink up to its height.

100.4 And in those days the Angels will come down into the hidden places, and gather together in one place all those who have helped sin, and the Most High will rise on that day to execute the Great Judgment on all the sinners.

100.5 And he will set guards, from the Holy Angels, over all the righteous and Holy, and they will guard them like the apple of an eye, until an end is made of all evil and all sin. And even if the righteous sleep a long sleep they have nothing to fear.

100.6 And the wise men will see the truth, and the sons of the Earth will understand all the words of this book, and they will know that their riches will not be able to save them or overthrow their sin.

100.7 Woe to you, you sinners, when you afflict the righteous on the day of severe trouble, and burn them with fire, you will be repaid according to your deeds.

100.8 Woe to you, you perverse of heart who watch to devise evil; fear will come upon you and there is no one who will help you.

100.9 Woe to you, you sinners, for an account of the words of your mouth, and for an account of the deeds of your hands that you have impiously done; you will burn in blazing flames of fire.

100.10 And now know that the Angels will inquire in Heaven into your deeds, from the Sun and the Moon and the Stars, into your sins, for on earth you execute judgment on the righteous.

100.11 And all the clouds and mist and dew and rain will testify against you, for they will be withheld from you so that they do not fall on you, and they will think about your sins.

100.12 And now give gifts to the rain, so that it may not be withheld from falling on you, and so that the dew, if it has accepted gold and silver from you, may fall.

100.13 When the hoarfrost and snow, with their cold, and all the snow-winds with their torments fall on you. In those days, you will not be able to stand before them.

101.1 Contemplate Heaven, all you sons of Heaven, and all the works of the Most High, and fear him, and do not do evil in front of Him.

101.2 If He closes the Windows of Heaven, and withholds the rain and the dew, so that it does not fall on the earth because of you, what will you do?

101.3 And if he sends his anger upon you, and upon all your deeds, will you not entreat him? For you speak proud and hard against his righteousness. And you will not have peace.

101.4 And do you not see the captains of the ships; how their ships are tossed by the waves and rocked by the winds and are in distress?

101.5 And because of this they are afraid, for all their good possessions that go out on the sea with them, and they think nothing good in their hearts, only that the sea will swallow them up, and that they will be destroyed in it.

101.6 Is not all the sea, and all its waters, and all its movement, the work of the Most High, and did he not seal all it's doings and bind it all with sand?

101.7 And at his rebuke it dries up and becomes afraid, and all its fish die, and everything in it; but you sinners who are on Earth do not fear him.

101.8 Did he not make Heaven, Earth, and everything that is in them? And who gave knowledge, and wisdom, to all things that move on the ground and in the sea?

101.9 And do not those captains of the ships fear the sea? Yet, sinners do not fear the Most High.

102.1 And in those days, if he brings a fierce fire upon you, where

will you flee, and where will you be safe? And when he utters his voice against you will you not be terrified and afraid?

102.2 And all the Lights will shake with great fear, and the whole Earth will be terrified, and will tremble and quail.

102.3 And all the Angels will carry out their commands, and will seek to hide from the One who is Great in Glory, and the children of the Earth will tremble and shake; and you sinners will be cursed forever and will not have peace.

102.4 Do not be afraid you souls of the righteous, and be hopeful, you who have died in righteousness.

102.5 And do not be sad that your souls have gone down into Sheol in sadness and that your bodies did not obtain during your life a reward in accordance with your goodness.

102.6 But when you die the sinners will say about you: "As we die, the righteous have also died, and of what use to them were their deeds?"

102.7 "Behold, like us they have died in sadness and in darkness, and what advantage do they have over us? From now on we are equal."

102.8 "And what will they receive and what will they see forever? For behold, they too have died, and from now on they will never again see the light."

102.9 And I say to you, you sinners: "You are content to eat and drink, and strip men naked, and steal, and sin, and acquire possessions, and see good days.

102.10 But you saw the righteous, how their end was peace, for no wrong was found in them until the day of their death."

102.11 "But they were destroyed and became as though they had not been and their souls went down to Sheol in distress."

103

103.1 And now I swear to you, the righteous, by His Great Glory and His Honour, and by His Magnificent Sovereignty, and by His Majesty: - I swear to you that I understand this mystery.

103.2 And I have read the Tablets of Heaven and seen the writing of the Holy Ones. And I found written and engraved in it, concerning them, that all good, and joy, and honour, have been made ready, and written down, for the spirits of those who died in righteousness.

103.3 And much good will be given to you in recompense for your toil and that your lot will be more excellent than the lot of the living.

103.4 And the spirits of you who have died in righteousness will live, and your spirits will rejoice and be glad, and the memory of them will remain in front of the Great One for all the generations of eternity. Therefore do not fear their abuse.

103.5 Woe to you, you sinners, when you die in your sin, and those who are like you say about you: "Blessed were the sinners they saw their days.

103.6 And now they have died in prosperity and wealth, distress and slaughter they did not see during their life, but they have died in glory, and judgment was not executed on them in their life."

103.7 Know that their souls will be made to go down into Sheol, they will

be wretched, and their distress will be great.

103.8 And in darkness, and in chains, and in burning flames, your spirits will come to the Great Judgment. And the Great Judgment will last for all generations, forever. Woe to you for you will not have peace.

103.9 Do not say, the righteous and the good who were alive; "In the days of our affliction we toiled laboriously, and saw every affliction, and met many evils. We were spent and became few and our spirit small.

103.10 We were destroyed and there was no one who helped us with words or with deeds. We were powerless and found nothing. We were tortured and destroyed and did not expect to see life from one day to the next.

103.11 We hoped to become the head but became the tail. We toiled and laboured, but were not masters of the fruits of our toil; we became food for the sinners, and the lawless made their yoke heavy upon us.

103.12 Those who hated us, those who goaded us, were masters of us. And to those who hated us we bowed our necks but they did not have mercy on us.

103.13 We sought to escape from them so that we might flee and be at rest. But we found no place where we might flee and be safe from them.

103.14 We complained about them to the rulers, in our distress, and cried out against those who devoured us, but they took no notice of our cries, and did not wish to listen to our voice.

103.15 And they helped those who plundered us and devoured us, and those who made us few, and they concealed their wrongdoing, and did not remove from us the yoke of those who devoured us, and scattered us, and killed us. And they concealed our slaughter and did not remember that they had raised their hands against us."

104.

104.1 I swear to you, you righteous, that in Heaven the Angels remember you for good in front of the Glory of the Great One, and that your names are written down in front of the Glory of the Great One.

104.2 Be hopeful! For you were formerly put to shame through evils and afflictions, but now you will shine like the Lights of Heaven, and will be seen, and the Gate of Heaven will be opened to you.

104.3 And persevere in your cry for judgment and it will appear to you, for justice will be exacted from the rulers for all your distress, and from all those who helped those who plundered you.

104.4 Be hopeful, and do not abandon your hope, for you will have great joy like the Angels of Heaven.

104.5 What will you have to do? You will not have to hide on the day of the Great Judgment, nor will you be found to be sinners. The Eternal Judgment will be upon you for all the generations of eternity.

104.6 And now do not be afraid, you righteous, when you see the sinners growing strong and prospering in their desires, and do not be associated with them but keep far away from their wrongdoing, for you will be associates of the Host of Heaven.

104.7 For you sinners say: "None of our sins will be inquired into and written down!" But they will write down your sins every day.

104.8 And now I show you that light and darkness, day and night, see all your sins.

104.9 Do not be impious in your hearts, and do not lie, and do not alter the words of truth, nor say that the words of the Holy and Great One are lies, and do not praise your idols. For all your lies, and all your impiety, lead not to righteousness but to great sin.

104.10 And now I know this mystery; that many sinners will alter and distort the words of truth, and speak evil words, and lie, and concoct great fabrications, and write books in their own words.

104.11 But when they write my words exactly in their languages, and do not alter or omit anything from my words, but write everything exactly, everything that I testified about before; then I know another mystery:

104.12 That books will be given to the righteous and wise and will be a source of joy and truth and much wisdom.

104.13 And books will be given to them, and they will believe in them and rejoice over them; and all the righteous who have learnt from them all the ways of truth will be glad.

105.

105.1 And in those days, says the Lord, they shall call and testify to the sons of the Earth about the wisdom in them. Show it to them for you are their leaders and the rewards will be over all the Earth.

105.2 For my son and I will join our-selves with them, forever, in the paths of uprightness during their lives. And you will have peace. Rejoice - you sons of uprightness! Amen

FRAGMENT OF THE BOOK OF NOAH

106.1 And after those days my son Methuselah chose a wife for his son Lamech and she became pregnant by him and bore a son.

106.2 And his body was white like snow, and red like the flower of a rose, and the hair of his head was white like wool. And his eyes were beautiful and when he opened his eyes he made the whole house bright, like the Sun, so that the whole house was exception-ally bright.

106.3 And when he was taken from the hand of the midwife he opened his mouth and spoke to the Lord of Right-eousness.

106.4 And his father Lamech was afraid of him, and fled, and went to his father Methuselah.

106.5 And he said to him: "I have be-gotten a strange son; he is not like a man but is like the children of the An-gels of Heaven, of a different type and not like us. And his eyes are like the rays of the Sun and his face glorious.

106.6 And it seems to me that he is not sprung from me but from the Angels and I am afraid that something ex-traordinary may be done on the earth in his days.

106.7 And now, my father, I am en-treating you and petitioning you, to go to our father Enoch, and learn from

him the truth, for his dwelling is with the Angels."

106.8 And when Methuselah heard the words of his son he came to me, at the ends of the Earth, for he had heard that I was there. And he cried out, and I heard his voice and went to him. And I said to him: "Behold I am here my son, for you have come to me."

106.9 And he answered me, and said: "Because of a great matter I have come to you, and because of a disturb-ing vision, have I come near.

106.10 And now hear me, my father, for a child has been born to my son Lamech, whose form and type are not like the type of a man. His colour is whiter than snow, and redder than the flower of the rose, and the hair of his head is whiter than white wool. And his eyes are like the rays of the Sun; and he opened his eyes and made the whole house bright.

106.11 And he was taken from the hand of the midwife, and he opened his mouth, and blessed the Lord of Heaven.

106.12 And his father Lamech was afraid and fled to me. And he does not believe he is sprung from him but thinks him to be from the Angels of Heaven. And behold, I have come to you, so that you may make known to me the truth."

106.13 And I, Enoch, answered and said to him: "The Lord will do new things on Earth, and this I have al-ready seen in a vision, and made known to you. For in the generation of my father, Jared, some from the height of Heaven transgressed the word of the Lord.

106.14 And behold, they commit sin and transgress the law, and have been promiscuous with women, and commit sin with them, and have married some of them, and have begotten children by them.

106.15 And there will be great destruction over the whole Earth, and there will be a deluge, and there will be great destruction for one year.

106.16 But this child, who has been born to you, will be left on the Earth, and his three sons will be saved with him. When all the men who are on the Earth die he and his sons will be saved. **106.17** They will beget on the Earth giants, not of spirit, but of flesh, and there will be great wrath on Earth, and the Earth will be cleansed of all corruption.

106.18 And now make known to your son Lamech that the one who has been born is truly his son. And call his name Noah, for he will be a remnant for you and he and his sons will be saved from the destruction which is coming on the earth because of all the sin and all the iniquity, which will be committed on the Earth in his days.

106.19 But after this, there will be yet greater iniquity than that which was committed on the earth before. For I know the mysteries of the Holy Ones, for the Lord showed them to me and made them known to me, and I read them in the Tablets of Heaven.

107.1 And I saw written on them, that generation upon generation will do wrong, until a generation of righteousness shall arise, and wrongdoing shall be destroyed, and sin shall depart from the earth, and everything good shall come upon it.

107.2 And now, my son, go, make known to your son Lamech, that this child that has been born, is truly his son, and this is no lie.

107.3 And when Methuselah had heard the words of his father Enoch - for he showed him everything which is secret - he returned, having seen him, and called the name of that child Noah; for he will comfort the Earth after all the destruction.

108.1 Another book which Enoch wrote for his son Methuselah and for those who should come after him and keep the law in the last days.

108.2 You who have observed, and are waiting in these days, until an end shall be made of those who do evil, and an end shall be made of the power of the wrongdoers.

108.3 Do indeed wait until sin shall pass away, for their names shall be erased from the Books of the Holy Ones, and their offspring will be destroyed forever. And their spirits will be killed, and they will cry out and moan in a chaotic desert place, and will burn in fire, for there is no Earth there.

108.4 And there I saw something like a cloud, which could not be discerned, for because of its depth I was not able to look into it. And the flames of a fire I saw, burning brightly, and things like bright mountains revolved and shook from side to side.

108.5 And I asked one of the Holy Angels, who were with me, and I said to him: "What is this bright place? For there is no sky, but only the flames of a burning fire, and the sounds of crying, and weeping, and moaning, and severe pain."

108.6 And he said to me: "This place which you see; here will be thrown the spirits of the sinners, and of the blasphemers, and of those who do evil. And of those who alter everything that the Lord has spoken through the mouths of the prophets about the things that shall be done.

108.7 For there are books, and records, about them in Heaven above so that the Angels may read them and know what is about to come upon the sinners. And upon the spirits of the humble, and of those who afflicted their bodies and were recompensed by God, and of those who were abused by evil men.

108.8 Those who loved God and did not love gold, or silver, or any possessions, but gave up their bodies to torment.

108.9 Those who, from the moment they existed, did not desire earthly food, but counted themselves as a breath which passes away, and kept to this. And the Lord tested them much, and their spirits were found pure, so that they might bless His Name."

108.10 And all their blessings I have recounted in the books, and he has assigned them their reward, for they were found to be such that they loved Heaven more than their life in the world. And although they were trampled underfoot by evil men, and had to listen to reviling and reproach from them, and were abused, yet they blessed their Lord.

108.11 And the Lord said: "And now I will call the spirits of the good, who are of the Generation of Light, and I will transform those who were born in darkness, who in the flesh were not recompensed with honour as was fitting to their faith.

108.12 And I will bring out into the shining light those who love my Holy Name and I will set each one on the throne of his honour."

108.13 And they will shine for times without number, for righteous is the Judgment of God, for with the faithful He will keep faith in the dwelling of upright paths.

108.14 And they will see those who were born in darkness thrown into the darkness while the righteous shine.

108.15 And the sinners will cry out as they see them shining but they themselves will go where days and times have been written down for them.

ENOCH 2

THE BOOK OF
THE SECRETS OF ENOCH

ALSO KNOWN AS SLAVONIC ENOCH

INTRODUCTION

THE SECOND BOOK OF ENOCH (usually abbreviated 2 Enoch, and otherwise variously known as Slavonic Enoch or The Secrets of Enoch) is a pseudepigraphic (a text whose claimed authorship is unfounded) of the Old Testament. It is usually considered to be part of the Apocalyptic literature. Late 1st century CE is the dating often preferred. The text has been preserved in full only in Slavonic, but in 2009 it was announced that Coptic fragments of the book had been identified. Greek is indicated as the language behind the Slavonic version. It is not regarded as scripture by Jews or any Christian group. It was rediscovered and published at the end of 19th century.

Most scholars consider 2 Enoch to be composed by an unknown Jewish sectarian group, while some authors think it is a 1st century Christian text. A very few scholars consider it a later Christian work. This article discusses 2 Enoch. It is distinct from the Book of Enoch, known as 1 Enoch. There is also an unrelated 3 Enoch. The numbering of these texts has been applied by scholars to distinguish the texts from one another.

Dates ranging from the 1st century BC to the 10th century CE have been proposed, with the late 1st century CE often preferred. The date of the text can be deduced solely on the basis of the internal evidence since the book has survived only in the medieval manuscripts (even if a reference of 2 Enoch could be find in Origen's De Principis i, 3:3). Composition shall be later than the Book of the Watchers in 1 Enoch (about III century BCE). The crucial arguments for the early dating of the text have very largely been linked to the themes of the Temple in Jerusalem and its ongoing practices and customs. Scholarly efforts have been in this respect mostly directed toward finding hints that the Sanctuary was still standing when the original text was composed. Scholars noted that the text gives no indication that the destruction of the Temple had already occurred at the time of the book's composition. Critical readers of the pseudepigraphic would have some difficulties finding any explicit expression of feelings of sadness or mourning about the loss of the sanctuary.

Affirmations of the value of animal sacrifice and Enoch's halakhic instructions found in 2 Enoch 59 also appear to be fashioned not in the "preservationist," mishnaic-like mode but rather as if they reflected sacrificial practices that still existed when the author was writing his book. The author tries legitimize the central place of worship, which through the reference to the place Ahuzan, which is a cryptic name for a Jewish Temple.

Scholars have also previously noted in the text some indications of the ongoing practice of pilgrimage to the central place of worship. These indications could be expected in a text written in the Alexandrian Diaspora. Thus in his instructions to the children, Enoch repeatedly encourages them to bring the gifts before the face of God for the remission of sins, a practice which appears to recall well-known sacrificial customs widespread in the Second Temple period. Further, the Slavonic apocalypse also contains a direct command to visit the Temple three times a day, an inconsistency if the sanctuary had been already destroyed.

CHAPTERS I- LXVIII

1.1 There was a wise man, a great artificer, and the Lord conceived love for him and received him, that he should behold the uppermost dwellings and be an eye-witness of the wise and great and inconceivable and immutable realm of God Almighty, of the very wonderful and glorious and bright and many-eyed station of the Lord's servants, and of the inaccessible throne of the Lord, and of the degrees and manifestations of the incorporeal hosts, and of the ineffable ministration of the multitude of the elements, and of the various apparition and inexpressible singing of the host of Cherubim, and of the boundless light.

1.2 At that time, he said, when my one hundred and sixty-fifth year was completed, I begat my son Mathusal (Methuselah).

1.3 After this too I lived two hundred years and completed of all the years of my life three hundred and sixty-five years.

1.4 On the first day of the month I was in my house alone and was resting on my bed and slept.

1.5 And when I was asleep, great distress came up into my heart, and I was weeping with my eyes in sleep, and I could not understand what this distress was, or what would happen to me.

1.6 And there appeared to me two men, exceeding big, so that I never saw such on earth; their faces were shining like the sun, their eyes too (were) like a burning light, and from their lips was fire coming forth with clothing and singing of various kinds in appearance purple, their wings brighter than gold, their hands whiter than snow.

1.7 They were standing at the head of my bed and began to call me by my name.

1.8 And I arose from my sleep and saw clearly those two men standing in front of me.

1.9 And I saluted them and was seized with fear and the appearance of my face was changed from terror, and those men said to me:

1.10 Have courage, Enoch, do not fear; the eternal God sent us to you, and lo! You shalt to-day ascend with us into heaven, and you shall tell your sons and all your household all that they shall do without you on earth in your house, and let no one seek you till the Lord return you to them.

1.11 And I made haste to obey them and went out from my house, and made to the doors, as it was ordered me, and summoned my sons Mathusal (Methuselah) and Regim and Gaidad and made known to them all the marvels those (men) had told me.

2 1. Listen to me, my children, I know not whither I go, or what will befall me; now therefore, my children, I tell you: turn not from God before the face of the vain, who made not

Heaven and earth, for these shall perish and those who worship them, and may the Lord make confident your hearts in the fear of him. And now, my children, let no one think to seek me, until the Lord return me to you.

3.1 It came to pass, when Enoch had told his sons, that the angels took him on to their wings and bore him up on to the first heaven and placed him on the clouds. And there I looked, and again I looked higher, and saw the ether, and they placed me on the first heaven and showed me a very great Sea, greater than the earthly sea.

4.1 They brought before my face the elders and rulers of the stellar orders, and showed me two hundred angels, who rule the stars and (their) services to the heavens, and fly with their wings and come round all those who sail.

5.1 And here I looked down and saw the treasure-houses of the snow, and the angels who keep their terrible store-houses, and the clouds whence they come out and into which they go.

6.1 They showed me the treasure-house of the dew, like oil of the olive, and the appearance of its form, as of all the flowers of the earth; further many angels guarding the treasure-houses of these (things), and how they are made to shut and open.

7.1 And those men took me and led me up on to the second heaven, and showed me darkness, greater than earthly darkness, and there I saw prisoners hanging, watched, awaiting the great and boundless judgment, and these angels (spirits) were dark-looking, more than earthly darkness, and incessantly making weeping through all hours.

7.2 And I said to the men who were with me: Wherefore are these incessantly tortured? They answered me: These are God's apostates, who obeyed not God's commands, but took counsel with their own will, and turned away with their prince, who also (is) fastened on the fifth heaven.

7.3 And I felt great pity for them, and they saluted me, and said to me: Man of God, pray for us to the Lord; and I answered to them: Who am I, a mortal man, that I should pray for angels (spirits)? Who knows whither I go, or what will befall me? Or who will pray for me?

8.1 And those men took me thence, and led me up on to the third heaven, and placed me there; and I looked downwards, and saw the produce of these places, such as has never been known for goodness.

8.2 And I saw all the sweet-flowering trees and beheld their fruits, which were sweetsmelling, and all the foods borne (by them) bubbling with fragrant exhalation.

8.3 And in the midst of the trees that of life, in that place whereon the Lord rests, when he goes up into paradise; and this tree is of ineffable goodness and fragrance, and adorned more than every existing thing; and on all sides (it is) in form gold-looking and ver-milion and fire-like and covers all, and it has produce from all fruits.

8.4 Its root is in the garden at the earth's end.

8.5 And paradise is between corrupti-bility and incorruptibility.

8.6 And two springs come out which send forth honey and milk, and their springs send forth oil and wine, and they separate into four parts, and go round with quiet course, and go down into the PARADISE OF EDEN, btween corruptibility and incorrupti-bility.

8.7 And thence they go forth along the earth, and have a revolution to thcir circle even as other elements.

8.8 And here there is no unfruitful tree, and every place is blessed.

8.9 And (there are) three hundred an-gels very bright, who keep the garden, and with incessant sweet singing and never-silent voices serve the Lord throughout all days and hours.

8.10 And I said: How very sweet is this place, and those men said to me:

9.1 This place, O Enoch, is prepared for the righteous, who endure all man-ner of offence from those that exasperate their souls, who avert their eyes from iniquity, and make right-eous judgment, and give bread to the hungering, and cover the naked with clothing, and raise up the fallen, and help injured orphans, and who walk without fault before the face of the Lord, and serve him alone, and for them is prepared this place for eternal inheritance.

10.1 And those two men led me up on to the Northern side, and showed me there a very terrible place, and (there were) all manner of tortures in that place: cruel darkness and unillu-mined gloom, and there is no light there, but murky fire constantly flam-ing aloft, and (there is) a fiery river coming forth, and that whole place is everywhere fire, and everywhere (there is) frost and ice, thirst and shiv-ering, while the bonds are very cruel, and the angels (spirits) fearful and merciless, bearing angry weapons, merciless torture, and I said:

10.2 Woe, woe, how very terrible is this place.

10.3 And those men said to me: This place, O Enoch, is prepared for those who dishonour God, who on earth practice sin against nature, which is child-corruption after the sodomitic fashion, magic-making, enchantments and devilish witchcrafts, and who boast of their wicked deeds, stealing, lies, calumnies, envy, rancour, forni-cation, murder, and who, accursed, steal the souls of men, who, seeing the poor take away their goods and them-selves wax rich, injuring them for other men's goods; who being able to satisfy the empty, made the hungering to die; being able to clothe, stripped the naked; and who knew not their cre-ator, and bowed to the soulless (and lifeless) gods, who cannot see nor hear, vain gods, (who also) built hewn images and bow down to unclean handiwork, for all these is prepared this place among these, for eternal in-heritance.

11.1 Those men took me, and led me up on to the fourth heaven, and showed me all the successive goings, and all the rays of the light of sun and moon.

11.2 And I measure their goings, and compared their light, and saw that the sun's light is greater than the moon's.

11.3 Its circle and the wheels on which it goes always, like the wind going past with very marvellous speed, and day and night it has no rest.

11.4 Its passage and return (are accompanied by) four great stars, (and) each star has under it a thousand stars, to the right of the sun's wheel, (and by) four to the left, each having under it a thousand stars, altogether eight thousand, issuing with the sun continually.

11.5 And by day fifteen myriads of angels attend it, and by night A thousand.

11.6 And six-winged ones issue with the angels before the sun's wheel into the fiery flames, and a hundred angels kindle the sun and set it alight.

12.1 And I looked and saw other flying elements of the sun, whose names (are) Phoenixes and Chalkydri, marvellous and wonderful, with feet and tails in the form of a lion, and a crocodile's head, their appearance (is) empurpled, like the rainbow; their size (is) nine hundred measures, their wings (are like) those of angels, each (has) twelve, and they attend and accompany the sun, bearing heat and dew, as it is ordered them from God.

12.2 Thus (the sun) revolves and goes, and rises under the heaven, and its course goes under the earth with the light of its rays incessantly.

13.1 Those men bore me away to the east, and placed me at the sun's gates, where the sun goes forth according to the regulation of the seasons and the circuit of the months of the whole year, and the number of the hours day and night.

13.2 And I saw six gates open, each gate having sixty-one stadia and A quarter of one stadium, and I measured (them) truly, and understood their size (to be) so much, through which the sun goes forth, and goes to the west, and is made even, and rises throughout all the months, and turns back again from the six gates according to the succession of the seasons; thus (the period) of the whole year is finished after the returns of the four seasons.

14.1 And again those men led me away to the western parts, and showed me six great gates open corresponding to the eastern gates, opposite to where the sun sets, according to the number of the days three hundred and sixty-five and A quarter.

14.2 Thus again it goes down to the western gates, (and) draws away its light, the greatness of its brightness, under the earth; for since the crown of its shining is in heaven with the Lord, and guarded by four hundred angels, while the sun goes round on wheel under the earth, and stands seven great hours in night, and spends half (its course) under the earth, when it comes to the eastern approach in the eighth hour of the night, it brings its lights, and the crown of shining, and the sun flames forth more than fire.

15.1 Then the elements of the sun, called Phoenixes and Chalkydri break into song, therefore every bird flutters with its wings, rejoicing at the giver of light, and they broke into song at the command of the Lord.

15.2 The giver of light comes to give brightness to the whole world, and the morning guard takes shape, which is the rays of the sun, and the sun of the earth goes out, and receives its brightness to light up the whole face of the earth, and they showed me this calculation of the sun's going.

15.3 And the gates which it enters, these are the great gates of the calculation of the hours of the year; for this reason the sun is a great creation, whose circuit (lasts) twenty-eight years, and begins again from the beginning.

16.1 Those men showed me the other course, that of the moon, twelve great gates, crowned from west to east, by which the moon goes in and out of the customary times.

16.2 It goes in at the first gate to the western places of the sun, by the first gates with (thirty)-one (days) exactly, by the second gates with thirty-one days exactly, by the third with thirty days exactly, by the fourth with thirty days exactly, by the fifth with thirty-one days exactly, by the sixth with thirty-one days exactly, by the seventh with thirty days exactly, by the eighth with thirtyone days perfectly, by the ninth with thirtyone days exactly, by the tenth with thirty days perfectly, by the eleventh with thirtyone days exactly, by the twelfth with twenty-eight days exactly.

16.3 And it goes through the western gates in the order and number of the eastern, and accomplishes the three hundred and sixtyfive and a quarter days of the solar year, while the lunar year has three hundred fiftyfour, and there are wanting (to it) twelve days of the solar circle, which are the lunar epacts of the whole year.

16.4 Thus, too, the great circle contains five hundred and thirty-two years.

16.5 The quarter (of a day) is omitted for three years, the fourth fulfills it exactly.

16.6 Therefore they are taken outside of heaven for three years and are not added to the number of days, because they change the time of the years to two new months towards completion, to two others towards diminution.

16.7 And when the western gates are finished, it returns and goes to the eastern to the lights, and goes thus day and night about the heavenly circles, lower than all circles, swifter than the heavenly winds, and spirits and elements and angels flying; each angel has six wings.

16.8 It has a sevenfold course in nineteen years.

17.1 In the midst of the heavens I saw armed soldiers, serving the Lord, with tympana and organs, with incessant voice, with sweet voice, with sweet and incessant (voice) and various singing, which it is impossible to describe, and (which) astonishes every mind, so wonderful and marvellous is the singing of those angels, and I was delighted listening to it.

18.1 The men took me on to the fifth heaven and placed me, and there I saw many and countless soldiers, called Grigori, of human appearance, and their size (was) greater than that of great giants and their faces withered, and the silence of their mouths perpetual, and their was no service on the fifth heaven, and I said to the men who were with me:

18.2 Wherefore are these very withered and their faces melancholy, and their mouths silent, and (wherefore) is there no service on this heaven?

18.3 And they said to me: These are the Grigori, who with their prince Satanail (Satan) rejected the Lord of light, and after them are those who are held in great darkness on the second heaven, and three of them went down on to earth from the Lord's throne, to the place Ermon, and broke through their vows on the shoulder of the hill Ermon and saw the daughters of men how good they are, and took to themselves wives, and befouled the earth with their deeds, who in all times of their age made lawlessness and mixing, and giants are born and marvellous big men and great enmity.

18.4 And therefore God judged them with great judgment, and they weep for their brethren and they will be punished on the Lord's great day.

18.5 And I said to the Grigori: I saw your brethren and their works, and their great torments, and I prayed for them, but the Lord has condemned them (to be) under earth till (the existing) heaven and earth shall end for ever.

18.6 And I said: Wherefore do you wait, brethren, and do not serve before the Lord's face, and have not put your services before the Lord's face, lest you anger your Lord utterly?

18.7 And they listened to my admonition, and spoke to the four ranks in heaven, and lo! As I stood with those two men four trumpets trumpeted together with great voice, and the Grigori broke into song with one voice, and their voice went up before the Lord pitifully and affectingly.

19.1 And thence those men took me and bore me up on to the sixth heaven, and there I saw seven bands of angels, very bright and very glorious, and their faces shining more than the sun's shining, glistening, and there is no difference in their faces, or behaviour, or manner of dress; and these make the orders, and learn the goings of the stars, and the alteration of the moon, or revolution of the sun, and the good government of the world.

19.2 And when they see evildoing they make commandments and instruction, and sweet and loud singing, and all (songs) of praise.

19.3 These are the archangels who are above angels, measure all life in heaven and on earth, and the angels who are (appointed) over seasons and years, the angels who are over rivers and sea, and who are over the fruits of the earth, and the angels who are over every grass, giving food to all, to every living thing, and the angels who write all the souls of men, and all their deeds, and their lives before the Lord's face; in their midst are six Phoenixes and six Cherubim and six six-winged ones continually with one voice singing one voice, and it is not possible to describe their singing, and they rejoice before the Lord at his footstool.

20.1 And those two men lifted me up thence on to the seventh heaven, and I saw there a very great light, and fiery troops of great archangels, incorporeal forces, and dominions, orders and governments, Cherubim and seraphim, thrones and manyeyed ones, nine regiments, the Ioanit stations of light, and I became afraid, and began to tremble with great terror, and those men took me, and led me after them, and said to me:

20.2 Have courage, Enoch, do not fear, and showed me the Lord from afar, sitting on His very high throne. For what is there on the tenth heaven, since the Lord dwells there?

20.3 On the tenth heaven is God, in the Hebrew tongue he is called Aravat. 4 And all the heavenly troops would come and stand on the ten steps according to their rank, and would bow down to the Lord, and would again go to their places in joy and felicity, singing songs in the boundless light with small and tender voices, gloriously serving him.

21.1 And the Cherubim and seraphim standing about the throne, the six-winged and many-eyed ones do not depart, standing before the Lord's face doing his will, and cover his whole throne, singing with gentle voice before the Lord's face: Holy, holy, holy, Lord Ruler of Sabaoth, heavens and earth are full of Your glory.

21.2 When I saw all these things, those men said to me: Enoch, thus far is it commanded us to journey with you, and those men went away from me and thereupon I saw them not.

21.3 And I remained alone at the end of the seventh heaven and became afraid, and fell on my face and said to myself: Woe is me, what has befallen me?

21.4 And the Lord sent one of his glorious ones, the archangel Gabriel, and (he) said to me: Have courage, Enoch, do not fear, arise before the Lord's face into eternity, arise, come with me.

21.5 And I answered him, and said in myself: My Lord, my soul is departed from me, from terror and trembling, and I called to the men who led me up to this place, on them I relied, and (it is) with them I go before the Lord's face.

21.6 And Gabriel caught me up, as a leaf caught up by the wind, and placed me before the Lord's face.

21.7 And I saw the eighth heaven, which is called in the Hebrew tongue Muzaloth, changer of the seasons, of drought, and of wet, and of the twelve constellations of the circle of the firmament, which are above the seventh heaven.

21.8 And I saw the ninth heaven, which is called in Hebrew Kuchavim, where are the heavenly homes of the twelve constellations of the circle of the firmament.

22.1 On the tenth heaven, (which is called) Aravoth, I saw the appearance of the Lord's face, like iron made to glow in fire, and brought out, emitting sparks, and it burns.

22.2 Thus (in a moment of eternity) I saw the Lord's face, but the Lord's face is ineffable, marvellous and very awful, and very, very terrible.

22.3 And who am I to tell of the Lord's unspeakable being, and of his very wonderful face? And I cannot tell the quantity of his many instructions, and various voices, the Lord's throne (is) very great and not made with hands, nor the quantity of those standing round him, troops of Cherubim and seraphim, nor their incessant singing, nor his immutable beauty, and who shall tell of the ineffable greatness of his glory.

22.4 And I fell prone and bowed down to the Lord, and the Lord with his lips said to me:

22.5 Have courage, Enoch, do not fear, arise and stand before my face into eternity.

22.6 And the archistratege Michael lifted me up, and led me to before the Lord's face.

22.7 And the Lord said to his servants tempting them: Let Enoch stand before my face into eternity, and the glorious ones bowed down to the Lord, and said: Let Enoch go according to Your word.

22.8 And the Lord said to Michael: Go and take Enoch from out (of) his earthly garments, and anoint him with my sweet ointment, and put him into the garments of My glory.

22.9 And Michael did thus, as the Lord told him. He anointed me, and dressed me, and the appearance of that ointment is more than the great light, and his ointment is like sweet dew, and its smell mild, shining like the sun's ray, and I looked at myself, and (I) was like (transfigured) one of his glorious ones.

22.10 And the Lord summoned one of his archangels by name Pravuil, whose knowledge was quicker in wisdom than the other archangels, who wrote all the deeds of the Lord; and the Lord said to Pravuil: Bring out the books from my store-houses, and a reed of quick-writing, and give (it) to Enoch, and deliver to him the choice and comforting books out of your hand.

23.1 And he was telling me all the works of heaven, earth and sea, and all the elements, their passages and goings, and the thunderings of the thunders, the sun and moon, the goings and changes of the stars, the seasons, years, days, and hours, the risings of the wind, the numbers of the angels, and the formation of their songs, and all human things, the tongue of every human song and life, the commandments, instructions, and sweet-voiced singings, and all things that it is fitting to learn.

23.2 And Pravuil told me: All the things that I have told you, we have written. Sit and write all the souls of mankind, however many of them are born, and the places prepared for them to eternity; for all souls are prepared to eternity, before the formation of the world.

23.3 And all double thirty days and thirty nights, and I wrote out all things exactly, and wrote three hundred and sixty-six books.

24.1 And the Lord summoned me, and said to me: Enoch, sit down on my left with Gabriel.

24.2 And I bowed down to the Lord, and the Lord spoke to me: Enoch, beloved, all (that) you see, all things that are standing finished I tell to you even before the very beginning, all that I created from non-being, and visible (physical) things from invisible (spiritual).

24.3 Hear, Enoch, and take in these my words, for not to My angels have I told my secret, and I have not told them their rise, nor my endless realm, nor have they understood my creating, which I tell you to-day.

24.4 For before all things were visible (physical), I alone used to go about in the invisible (spiritual) things, like the sun from east to west, and from west to east.

24.5 But even the sun has peace in itself, while I found no peace, because I was creating all things, and I conceived the thought of placing

foundations, and of creating visible (physical) creation.

25.1 I commanded in the very lowest (parts), that visible (physical) things should come down from invisible (spiritual), and Adoil came down very great, and I beheld him, and lo! He had a belly of great light.

25.2 And I said to him: Become undone, Adoil, and let the visible (physical) (come) out of you.

25.3 And he came undone, and a great light came out. And I (was) in the midst of the great light, and as there is born light from light, there came forth a great age, and showed all creation, which I had thought to create.

25.4 And I saw that (it was) good.

25.5 And I placed for myself a throne, and took my seat on it, and said to the light: Go thence up higher and fix yourself high above the throne, and be A foundation to the highest things.

25.6 And above the light there is nothing else, and then I bent up and looked up from my throne.

26.1 And I summoned the very lowest a second time, and said: Let Archas come forth hard, and he came forth hard from the invisible (spiritual).

26.2 And Archas came forth, hard, heavy, and very red.

26.3 And I said: Be opened, Archas, and let there be born from you, and he came undone, an age came forth, very great and very dark, bearing the creation of all lower things, and I saw that (it was) good and said to him:

26.4 Go thence down below, and make yourself firm, and be a foundation for the lower things, and it happened and he went down and fixed himself, and became the foundation for the lower things, and below the darkness there is nothing else.

27.1 And I commanded that there should be taken from light and darkness, and I said: Be thick, and it became thus, and I spread it out with the light, and it became water, and I spread it out over the darkness, below the light, and then I made firm the waters, that is to say the bottomless, and I made foundation of light around the water, and created seven circles from inside, and imaged (the water) like crystal wet and dry, that is to say like glass, (and) the circumcession of the waters and the other elements, and I showed each one of them its road, and the seven stars each one of them in its heaven, that they go thus, and I saw that it was good.

27.2 And I separated between light and between darkness, that is to say in the midst of the water hither and thither, and I said to the light, that it should be the day, and to the darkness, that it should be the night, and there was evening and there was morning the first day.

28.1 And then I made firm the heavenly circle, and (made) that the lower water which is under heaven collect itself together, into one whole, and that the chaos become dry, and it became so.

28.2 Out of the waves I created rock hard and big, and from the rock I piled up the dry, and the dry I called earth, and the midst of the earth I called abyss, that is to say the bottomless, I collected the sea in one place and bound it together with a yoke.

28.3 And I said to the sea: Behold I give you (your) eternal limits, and you shalt not break loose from your component parts.

28.4 Thus I made fast the firmament. This day I called me the first-created [Sunday].

29.1 And for all the heavenly troops I imaged the image and essence of fire, and my eye looked at the very hard, firm rock, and from the gleam of my eye the lightning received its wonderful nature, (which) is both fire in water and water in fire, and one does not put out the other, nor does the one dry up the other, therefore the lightning is brighter than the sun, softer than water and firmer than hard rock.

29.2 And from the rock I cut off a great fire, and from the fire I created the orders of the incorporeal ten troops of angels, and their weapons are fiery and their raiment a burning flame, and I commanded that each one should stand in his order.

29.3 And one from out the order of angels, having turned away with the order that was under him, conceived an impossible thought, to place his throne higher than the clouds above the earth, that he might become equal in rank to my power.

29.4 And I threw him out from the height with his angels, and he was flying in the air continuously above the bottomless.

30.1 On the third day I commanded the earth to make grow great and fruitful trees, and hills, and seed to sow, and I planted Paradise, and enclosed it, and placed as armed (guardians) flaming angels, and thus I created renewal.

30.2 Then came evening, and came morning the fourth day.

30.3 [Wednesday]. On the fourth day I commanded that there should be great lights on the heavenly circles.

30.4 On the first uppermost circle I placed the stars, Kruno, and on the second Aphrodit, on the third Aris, on the fifth Zoues, on the sixth Ermis, on the seventh lesser the moon, and adorned it with the lesser stars.

30.5 And on the lower I placed the sun for the illumination of day, and the moon and stars for the illumination of night.

30.6 The sun that it should go according to each constellation, twelve, and I appointed the succession of the months and their names and lives, their thunderings, and their hourmarkings, how they should succeed.

30.7 Then evening came and morning came the fifth day.

30.8 [Thursday]. On the fifth day I commanded the sea, that it should bring forth fishes, and feathered birds of many varieties, and all animals creeping over the earth, going forth over the earth on four legs, and soaring in the air, male sex and female, and every soul breathing the spirit of life.

30.9 And there came evening, and there came morning the sixth day.

30.10 [Friday]. On the sixth day I commanded my wisdom to create man from seven consistencies: one, his flesh from the earth; two, his blood from the dew; three, his eyes from the sun; four, his bones from stone; five, his intelligence from the swiftness of the angels and from cloud; six, his veins and his hair from the grass of the earth; seven, his soul from my breath and from the wind.

30.11 And I gave him seven natures: to the flesh hearing, the eyes for sight, to the soul smell, the veins for touch, the blood for taste, the bones for endurance, to the intelligence sweetness [enjoyment].

30.12 I conceived a cunning saying to say, I created man from invisible (spiritual) and from visible (physical) nature, of both are his death and life and image, he knows speech like some created thing, small in greatness and again great in smallness, and I placed him on earth, a second angel, honourable, great and glorious, and I appointed him as ruler to rule on earth and to have my wisdom, and there was none like him of earth of all my existing creatures.

30.13 And I appointed him a name, from the four component parts, from east, from west, from south, from north, and I appointed for him four special stars, and I called his name Adam, and showed him the two ways, the light and the darkness, and I told him:

30.14 This is good, and that bad, that I should learn whether he has love towards me, or hatred, that it be clear which in his race love me.

30.15 For I have seen his nature, but he has not seen his own nature, therefore (through) not seeing he will sin worse, and I said After sin (what is there) but death?

30.16 And I put sleep into him and he fell asleep. And I took from him A rib, and created him a wife, that death should come to him by his wife, and I took his last word and called her name mother, that is to say, Eva (Eve).

31.1 Adam has life on earth, and I created a garden in Eden in the east, that he should observe the testament and keep the command.

31.2 I made the heavens open to him, that he should see the angels singing the song of victory, and the gloomless light.

31.3 And he was continuously in paradise, and the devil understood that I wanted to create another world, because Adam was lord on earth, to rule and control it.

31.4 The devil is the evil spirit of the lower places, as a fugitive he made Sotona from the heavens as his name was Satanail (Satan), thus he became different from the angels, (but his nature) did not change (his) intelligence as far as (his) understanding of righteous and sinful (things).

31.5 And he understood his condemnation and the sin which he had sinned before, therefore he conceived thought against Adam, in such form he entered and seduced Eva (Eve), but did not touch Adam.

31.6 But I cursed ignorance, but what I had blessed previously, those I did not curse, I cursed not man, nor the earth, nor other creatures, but man's evil fruit, and his works.

32.1 I said to him: Earth you are, and into the earth whence I took you you shalt go, and I will not ruin you, but send you whence I took you.

32.2 Then I can again receive you at My second presence.

32.3 And I blessed all my creatures visible (physical) and invisible (spiritual). And Adam was five and half hours in paradise.

32.4 And I blessed the seventh day, which is the Sabbath, on which he rested from all his works.

33.1 And I appointed the eighth day also, that the eighth day should be the firstcreated after my work, and that (the first seven) revolve in the form of the seventh thousand, and that at the beginning of the eighth thousand there should be a time of not-counting, endless, with neither years nor months nor weeks nor days nor hours.

33.2 And now, Enoch, all that I have told you, all that you have understood, all that you have seen of heavenly things, all that you have seen on earth, and all that I have written in books by my great wisdom, all these things I have devised and created from the uppermost foundation to the lower and to the end, and there is no counsellor nor inheritor to my creations.

33.3 I am self-eternal, not made with hands, and without change.

33.4 My thought is my counsellor, my wisdom and my word are made, and my eyes observe all things how they stand here and tremble with terror.

33.5 If I turn away my face, then all things will be destroyed.

33.6 And apply your mind, Enoch, and know him who is speaking to you, and take thence the books which you yourself have written.

33.7 And I give you Samuil and Raguil, who led you up, and the books, and go down to earth, and tell your sons all that I have told you, and all that you have seen, from the lower heaven up to my throne, and all the troops.

33.8 For I created all forces, and there is none that resists me or that does not subject himself to me. For all subject themselves to my monarchy, and labour for my sole rule.

33.9 Give them the books of the handwriting, and they will read (them) and will know me for the creator of all things, and will understand how there is no other God but me.

33.10 And let them distribute the books of your handwriting–children to children, generation to generation, nations to nations.

33.11 And I will give you, Enoch, my intercessor, the archistratege Michael, for the handwritings of your fathers Adam, Seth, Enos, Cainan, Mahaleleel, and Jared your father.

34.1 They have rejected my commandments and my yoke, worthless seed has come up, not fearing God, and they would not bow down to me, but have begun to bow down to vain gods, and denied my unity, and have laden the whole earth with untruths, offences, abominable lecheries, namely one with another, and all manner of other unclean wickedness, which are disgusting to relate.

34.2 And therefore I will bring down a deluge upon the earth and will destroy all men, and the whole earth will crumble together into great darkness.

35.1 Behold from their seed shall arise another generation, much afterwards, but of them many will be very insatiate.

35.2 He who raises that generation, (shall) reveal to them the books of your handwriting, of your fathers, (to them) to whom he must point out the guardianship of the world, to the faithful men and workers of my pleasure, who do not acknowledge my name in vain.

35.3 And they shall tell another generation, and those (others) having read shall be glorified thereafter, more than the first.

36.1 Now, Enoch, I give you the term of thirty days to spend in your house, and tell your sons and all your household, that all may hear from my face what is told them by you, that they may read and understand, how there is no other God but me.

36.2 And that they may always keep my commandments, and begin to read and take in the books of your handwriting.

36.3 And after thirty days I shall send my angel for you, and he will take you from earth and from your sons to me.

37.1 And the Lord called upon one of the older angels, terrible and menacing, and placed him by me, in appearance white as snow, and his hands like ice, having the appearance of great frost, and he froze my face, because I could not endure the terror of the Lord, just as it is not possible to endure A stove's fire and the sun's heat, and the frost of the air.

37.2 And the Lord said to me: Enoch, if your face be not frozen here, no man will be able to behold your face.

38.1 And the Lord said to those men who first led me up: Let Enoch go down on to earth with you, and await him till the determined day.

38.2 And they placed me by night on my bed.

38.3 And Mathusal (Methuselah) expecting my coming, keeping watch by day and by night at my bed, was filled with awe when he heard my coming, and I told him, Let all my household come together, that I tell them everything.

39.1 Oh my children, my beloved ones, hear the admonition of your father, as much as is according to the Lord's will.

39.2 I have been let come to you today, and announce to you, not from my lips, but from the Lord's lips, all that is and was and all that is now, and all that will be till judgment-day.

39.3 For the Lord has let me come to you, you hear therefore the words of my lips, of a man made big for you, but I am one who has seen the Lord's face, like iron made to glow from fire it sends forth sparks and burns.

39.4 You look now upon my eyes, (the eyes) of a man big with meaning for you, but I have seen the Lord's eyes, shining like the sun's rays and filling the eyes of man with awe.

39.5 You see now, my children, the right hand of a man that helps you, but I have seen the Lord's right hand filling heaven as he helped me.

39.6 You see the compass of my work like your own, but I have seen the Lord's limitless and perfect compass, which has no end.

39.7 You hear the words of my lips, as I heard the words of the Lord, like great thunder incessantly with hurling of clouds.

39.8 And now, my children, hear the discourses of the father of the earth, how fearful and awful it is to come before the face of the ruler of the earth, how much more terrible and awful it is to come before the face of the ruler of heaven, the controller (judge) of quick and dead, and of the heavenly troops. Who can endure that endless pain?

40.1 And now, my children, I know all things, for this (is) from the Lord's lips, and this my eyes have seen, from beginning to end.

40.2 I know all things, and have written all things into books, the heavens and their end, and their plenitude, and all the armies and their marchings.

40.3 I have measured and described the stars, the great countless multitude (of them).

40.4 What man has seen their revolutions, and their entrances? For not even the angels see their number, while I have written all their names.

40.5 And I measured the sun's circle, and measured its rays, counted the hours, I wrote down too all things that go over the earth, I have written the things that are nourished, and all seed sown and unsown, which the earth produces and all plants, and every grass and every flower, and their sweet smells, and their names, and the dwellingplaces of the clouds, and their composition, and their wings, and how they bear rain and raindrops.

40.6 And I investigated all things, and wrote the road of the thunder and of the lightning, and they showed me the keys and their guardians, their rise, the way they go; it is let out (gently) in measure by a chain, lest by A heavy chain and violence it hurl down the angry clouds and destroy all things on earth.

40.7 I wrote the treasure-houses of the snow, and the store-houses of the cold and the frosty airs, and I observed their season's key-holder, he fills the clouds with them, and does not exhaust the treasure-houses.

40.8 And I wrote the resting-places of the winds and observed and saw how their keyholders bear weighing-scales and measures; first, they put them in (one) weighing-scale, then in the other the weights and let them out according to measure cunningly over the whole earth, lest by heavy breathing they make the earth to rock.

40.9 And I measured out the whole earth, its mountains, and all hills, fields, trees, stones, rivers, all existing things I wrote down, the height from earth to the seventh heaven, and downwards to the very lowest hell, and the judgment-place, and the very great, open and weeping hell.

40.10 And I saw how the prisoners are in pain, expecting the limitless judgment.

40.11 And I wrote down all those being judged by the judge, and all their judgment (and sentences) and all their works.

41.1 And I saw all forefathers from (all) time with Adam and Eva (Eve), and I sighed and broke into tears and said of the ruin of their dishonour:

41.2 Woe is me for my infirmity and (for that) of my forefathers, and thought in my heart and said:

41.2 Blessed (is) the man who has not been born or who has been born and shall not sin before the Lord's face, that he come not into this place, nor bring the yoke of this place.

42.1 I saw the key-holders and guards of the gates of hell standing, like great serpents, and their faces like extinguishing lamps, and their eyes of fire, their sharp teeth, and I saw all the Lord's works, how they are right, while the works of man are some (good), and others bad, and in their works are known those who lie evilly.

43.1 I, my children, measured and wrote out every work and every measure and every righteous judgment.

43.2 As (one) year is more honourable than another, so is (one) man more honourable than another, some for great possessions, some for wisdom of heart, some for particular intellect, some for cunning, one for silence of lip, another for cleanliness, one for strength, another for comeliness, one for youth, another for sharp wit, one for shape of body, another for sensibility, let it be heard everywhere, but there is none better than he who fears God, he shall be more glorious in time to come.

44.1 The Lord with his hands having created man, in the likeness of his own face, the Lord made him small and great.

44.2 Whoever reviles the ruler's face, and abhors the Lord's face, has despised the Lord's face, and he who vents anger on any man without injury, the Lord's great anger will cut him down, he who spits on the face of man reproachfully, will be cut down at the Lord's great judgment.

44.3 Blessed is the man who does not direct his heart with malice against any man, and helps the injured and condemned, and raises the broken down, and shall do charity to the needy, because on the day of the great judgment every weight, every measure and every makeweight (will be) as in the market, that is to say (they are) hung on scales and stand in the market, (and every one) shall learn his own measure, and according to his measure shall take his reward.

45.1 Whoever hastens to make offerings before the Lord's face, the Lord for his part will hasten that offering by granting of his work.

45.2 Buwhoever increases his lamp before the Lord's face and make not true judgment, the Lord will (not) increase his treasure in the realm of the highest.

45.3 When the Lord demands bread, or candles, or (the)flesh (of beasts), or any other sacrifice, then that is nothing; but God demands pure hearts, and with all that (only) tests the heart of man.

46.1 Hear, my people, and take in the words of my lips.

46.2 If any one bring any gifts to an earthly ruler, and have disloyal thoughts in his heart, and the ruler know this, will he not be angry with him, and not refuse his gifts, and not give him over to judgment?

46.3 Or (if) one man make himself appear good to another by deceit of tongue, but (have) evil in his heart, then will not (the other) understand the treachery of his heart, and himself be condemned, since his untruth was plain to all?

46.4 And when the Lord shall send a great light, then there will be judgment for the just and the unjust, and there no one shall escape notice.

47.1 And now, my children, lay thought on your hearts, mark well the words of your father, which are all (come) to you from the Lord's lips.

47.2 Take these books of your father's handwriting and read them.

47.3 For the books are many, and in them you will learn all the Lord's works, all that has been from the beginning of creation, and will be till the end of time.

47.4 And if you will observe my handwriting, you will not sin against the Lord; because there is no other except the Lord, neither in heaven, nor in earth, nor in the very lowest (places), nor in the (one) foundation.

47.5 The Lord has placed the foundations in the unknown, and has spread forth heavens visible (physical) and invisible (spiritual); he fixed the earth on the waters, and created countless creatures, and who has counted the water and the foundation of the unfixed, or the dust of the earth, or the sand of the sea, or the drops of the rain, or the morning dew, or the wind's breathings? Who has filled earth and sea, and the indissoluble winter?

47.6 I cut the stars out of fire, and decorated heaven, and put it in their midst.

48.1 That the sun go along the seven heavenly circles, which are the appointment of one hundred and eighty-two thrones, that it go down on a short day, and again one hundred and eighty-two, that it go down on a big day, and he has two thrones on which he rests, revolving hither and thither above the thrones of the months, from the seventeenth day of the month Tsivan it goes down to the month Thevan, from the seventeenth of Thevan it goes up.

48.2 And thus it goes close to the earth, then the earth is glad and makes grow its fruits, and when it goes away, then the earth is sad, and trees and all fruits have no florescence.

48.3 All this he measured, with good measurement of hours, and fixed A measure by his wisdom, of the visible (physical) and the invisible (spiritual).

48.4 From the invisible (spiritual) he made all things visible (physical), himself being invisible (spiritual).

48.5 Thus I make known to you, my children, and distribute the books to your children, into all your generations, and amongst the nations who shall have the sense to fear God, let them receive them, and may they come to love them more than any food or earthly sweets, and read them and apply themselves to them.

48.6 And those who understand not the Lord, who fear not God, who accept not, but reject, who do not receive the (books), a terrible judgment awaits these.

48.7 Blessed is the man who shall bear their yoke and shall drag them along, for he shall be released on the day of the great judgment.

49.1 I swear to you, my children, but I swear not by any oath, neither by heaven nor by earth, nor by any other creature which God created.

49.2 The Lord said: There is no oath in me, nor injustice, but truth.

49.3 If there is no truth in men, let them swear by the words, Yea, yea, or else, Nay, nay.

49.4 And I swear to you, yea, yea, that there has been no man in his mother's womb, (but that) already before, even to each one there is a place prepared for the repose of that soul, and a measure fixed how much it is intended that a man be tried in this world.

49.5 Yea, children, deceive not yourselves, for there has been previously prepared a place for every soul of man.

50.1 I have put every man's work in writing and none born on earth can remain hidden nor his works remain concealed.

50.2 I see all things.

50.3 Now therefore, my children, in patience and meekness spend the number of your days, that you inherit endless life.

50.4 Endure for the sake of the Lord every wound, every injury, every evil word and attack.

50.5 If ill-requitals befall you, return (them) not either to neighbour or enemy, because the Lord will return (them) for you and be your avenger on the day of great judgment, that there be no avenging here among men.

50.6 Whoever of you spends gold or silver for his brother's sake, he will receive ample treasure in the world to come.

50.7 Injure not widows nor orphans nor strangers, lest God's wrath come upon you.

51.1 Stretch out your hands to the poor according to your strength.

51.2 Hide not your silver in the earth.

51.3 Help the faithful man in affliction, and affliction will not find you in the time of your trouble.

51.4 And every grievous and cruel yoke that come upon you bear all for the sake of the Lord, and thus you will find your reward in the day of judgment.

51.5 It is good to go morning, midday, and evening into the Lord's dwelling, for the glory of your creator.

51.6 Because every breathing (thing) glorifies him, and every creature visible (physical) and invisible (spiritual) returns him praise.

52.1 Blessed is the man who opens his lips in praise of God of Sabaoth and praises the Lord with his heart.

52.2 Cursed every man who opens his lips for the bringing into contempt and calumny of his neighbour, because he brings God into contempt.

52.3 Blessed is he who opens his lips blessing and praising God.

52.4 Cursed is he before the Lord all the days of his life, who opens his lips to curse and abuse.

52.5 Blessed is he who blesses all the Lord's works.

52.6 Cursed is he who brings the Lord's creation into contempt.

52.7 Blessed is he who looks down and raises the fallen.

52.8 Cursed is he who looks to and is eager for the destruction of what is not his.

52.9 Blessed is he who keeps the foundations of his fathers made firm from the beginning.

52.10 Cursed is he who perverts the decrees of his forefathers.

52.11 Blessed is he who imparts peace and love.

52.12 Cursed is he who disturbs those that love their neighbours.

52.13 Blessed is he who speaks with humble tongue and heart to all.

52.14 Cursed is he who speaks peace with his tongue, while in his heart there is no peace but a sword.

52.15 For all these things will be laid bare in the weighing-scales and in the books, on the day of the great judgment.

53.1 And now, my children, do not say:

Our father is standing before God, and is praying for our sins, for there is there no helper of any man who has sinned.

53.2 You see how I wrote all works of every man, before his creation, (all) that is done amongst all men for all time, and none can tell or relate my handwriting, because the Lord see all imaginings of man, how they are vain, where they lie in the treasurehouses of the heart.

53.3 And now, my children, mark well all the words of your father, that I tell you, lest you regret, saying: Why did our father not tell us?

54.1 At that time, not understanding this let these books which I have given you be for an inheritance of your peace.

54.2 Hand them to all who want them, and instruct them, that they may see the Lord's very great and marvellous works.

55.1 My children, behold, the day of my term and time have approached.

55.2 For the angels who shall go with me are standing before me and urge me to my departure from you; they are standing here on earth, awaiting what has been told them.

55.3 For to-morrow I shall go up on to heaven, to the uppermost Jerusalem to my eternal inheritance.

55.4 Therefore I bid you do before the Lord's face all (his) good pleasure.

56.1 Mathosalam having answered his father Enoch, said: What is agreeable to your eyes, father, that I may make before your face, that you may bless our dwellings, and your sons, and that your people may be made glorious through you, and then (that) you may depart thus, as the Lord said?

56.2 Enoch answered to his son Mathosalam (and) said: Hear, child, from the time when the Lord anointed me with the ointment of his glory, (there has been no) food in me, and my soul remembers not earthly enjoyment, neither do I want anything earthly.

57.1 My child Methosalam, summon all your brethren and all your household and the elders of the people, that I may talk to them and depart, as is planned for me.

57.2 And Methosalam made haste, and summoned his brethren, Regim,

Riman, Uchan, Chermion, Gaidad, and all the elders of the people before the face of his father Enoch; and he blessed them, (and) said to them:

58.1 Listen to me, my children, today.

58.2 In those days when the Lord came down on to earth for Adam's sake, and visited all his creatures, which he created himself, after all these he created Adam, and the Lord called all the beasts of the earth, all the reptiles, and all the birds that soar in the air, and brought them all before the face of our father Adam.

58.3 And Adam gave the names to all things living on earth.

58.4 And the Lord appointed him ruler over all, and subjected to him all things under his hands, and made them dumb and made them dull that they be commanded of man, and be in subjection and obedience to him.

58.5 Thus also the Lord created every man lord over all his possessions.

58.6 The Lord will not judge a single soul of beast for man's sake, but adjudges the souls of men to their beasts in this world; for men have a special place.

58.7 And as every soul of man is according to number, similarly beasts will not perish, nor all souls of beasts which the Lord created, till the great judgment, and they will accuse man, if he feed them ill.

59.1 Whoever defiles the soul of beasts, defiles his own soul.

59.2 For man brings clean animals to make sacrifice for sin, that he may have cure of his soul.

59.3 And if they bring for sacrifice clean animals, and birds, man has cure, he cures his soul.

59.4 All is given you for food, bind it by the four feet, that is to make good the cure, he cures his soul.

59.5 But whoever kills beast without wounds, kills his own souls and defiles his own flesh.

59.6 And he who does any beast any injury whatsoever, in secret, it is evil practice, and he defiles his own soul.

60.1 He who works the killing of a man's soul, kills his own soul, and kills his own body, and there is no cure for him for all time.

60.2 He who puts a man in any snare, shall stick in it himself, and there is no cure for him for all time.

60.3 He who puts a man in any vessel, his retribution will not be wanting at the great judgment for all time.

60.4 He who works crookedly or speaks evil against any soul, will not make justice for himself for all time.

61.1 And now, my children, keep your hearts from every injustice, which the Lord hates. Just as a man asks something for his own soul from God, so let him do to every living soul, because I know all things, how in the great time to come there is much inheritance prepared for men, good for the good, and bad for the bad, without number many.

61.2 Blessed are those who enter the good houses, for in the bad houses there is no peace nor return from them.
61.3 Hear, my children, small and great! When man puts a good thought in his heart, brings gifts from his labours before the Lord's face and his hands made them not, then the Lord will turn away his face from the labour of his hand, and (that) man cannot find the labour of his hands.
61.4 And if his hands made it, but his heart murmur, and his heart cease not making murmur incessantly, he has not any advantage.

62.1 Blessed is the man who in his patience brings his gifts with faith before the Lord's face, because he will find forgiveness of sins.
62.2 But if he take back his words before the time, there is no repentance for him; and if the time pass and he do not of his own will what is promised, there is no repentance after death.
62.3 Because every work which man does before the time, is all deceit before men, and sin before God.

63.1 When man clothes the naked and fills the hungry, he will find reward from God.
63.2 But if his heart murmur, he commits a double evil; ruin of himself and of that which he gives; and for him there will be no finding of reward on account of that.
63.3 And if his own heart is filled with his food and his own flesh, clothed with his own clothing, he commits

contempt, and will forfeit all his endurance of poverty, and will not find reward of his good deeds.
64.4 Every proud and magniloquent man is hateful to the Lord, and every false speech, clothed in untruth; it will be cut with the blade of the sword of death, and thrown into the fire, and shall burn for all time.

64.1 When Enoch had spoken these words to his sons, all people far and near heard how the Lord was calling Enoch. They took counsel together:
64.2 Let us go and kiss Enoch, and two thousand men came together and came to the place Achuzan where Enoch was, and his sons.
64.3 And the elders of the people, the whole assembly, came and bowed down and began to kiss Enoch and said to him:
64.4 Our father Enoch, (may) you (be) blessed of the Lord, the eternal ruler, and now bless your sons and all the people, that we may be glorified today before your face.
64.5 For you shalt be glorified before the Lord's face for all time, since the Lord chose you, rather than all men on earth, and designated you writer of all his creation, visible (physical) and invisible (spiritual), and redeemed of the sins of man, and helper of your household.

65.1 And Enoch answered all his people saying: Hear, my children, before that all creatures were created, the Lord created the visible (physical) and invisible (spiritual) things.

65.2 And as much time as there was and went past, understand that after all that he created man in the likeness of his own form, and put into him eyes to see, and ears to hear, and heart to reflect, and intellect wherewith to deliberate.

65.3 And the Lord saw all man's works, and created all his creatures, and divided time, from time he fixed the years, and from the years he appointed the months, and from the months he appointed the days, and of days he appointed seven.

65.4 And in those he appointed the hours, measured them out exactly, that man might reflect on time and count years, months, and hours, (their) alternation, beginning, and end, and that he might count his own life, from the beginning until death, and reflect on his sin and write his work bad and good; because no work is hidden before the Lord, that every man might know his works and never transgress all his commandments, and keep my handwriting from generation to generation.

65.5 When all creation visible (physical) and invisible (spiritual), as the Lord created it, shall end, then every man goes to the great judgment, and then all time shall perish, and the years, and thenceforward there will be neither months nor days nor hours, they will be adhered together and will not be counted.

65.6 There will be one aeon, and all the righteous who shall escape the Lord's great judgment, shall be collected in the great aeon, for the righteous the great aeon will begin, and they will live eternally, and then

too there will be amongst them neither labour, nor sickness, nor humiliation, nor anxiety, nor need, nor brutality, nor night, nor darkness, but great light.

65.7 And they shall have a great indestructible wall, and a paradise bright and incorruptible (eternal), for all corruptible (mortal) things shall pass away, and there will be eternal life.

66.1 And now, my children, keep your souls from all injustice, such as the Lord hates.

66.2 Walk before his face with terror and trembling and serve him alone.

66.3 Bow down to the true God, not to dumb idols, but bow down to his similitude, and bring all just offerings before the Lord's face. The Lord hates what is unjust.

66.4 For the Lord sees all things; when man takes thought in his heart, then he counsels the intellects, and every thought is always before the Lord, who made firm the earth and put all creatures on it.

66.5 If you look to heaven, the Lord is there; if you take thought of the sea's deep and all the under-earth, the Lord is there.

66.6 For the Lord created all things. Bow not down to things made by man, leaving the Lord of all creation, because no work can remain hidden before the Lord's face.

66.7 Walk, my children, in long-suffering, in meekness, honesty, in provocation, in grief, in faith and in truth, in (reliance on) promises, in illness, in abuse, in wounds, in temptation, in nakedness, in privation, loving one another, till you go out from this age of ills, that you become inheritors of endless time.

66.8 Blessed are the just who shall escape the great judgment, for they shall shine forth more than the sun sevenfold, for in this world the seventh part is taken off from all, light, darkness, food, enjoyment, sorrow, paradise, torture, fire, frost, and other things; he put all down in writing, that you might read and understand.

67.1 When Enoch had talked to the people, the Lord sent out darkness on to the earth, and there was darkness, and it covered those men standing with Enoch, and they took Enoch up on to the highest heaven, where the Lord (is); and he received him and placed him before his face, and the darkness went off from the earth, and light came again.

67.2 And the people saw and understood not how Enoch had been taken, and glorified God, and found a roll in which was traced The Invisible (spiritual) God; and all went to their dwelling places.

68.1 Enoch was born on the sixth day of the month Tsivan, and lived three hundred and sixty-five years.

68.2 He was taken up to heaven on the first day of the month Tsivan and remained in heaven sixty days.

68.3 He wrote all these signs of all creation, which the Lord created, and wrote three hundred and sixty-six books, and handed them over to his sons and remained on earth thirty days, and was again taken up to heaven on the sixth day of the month Tsivan, on the very day and hour when he was born.

68.4 As every man's nature in this life is dark, so are also his conception, birth, and departure from this life.

68.5 At what hour he was conceived, at that hour he was born, and at that hour too he died.

68.6 Methosalam and his brethren, all the sons of Enoch, made haste, and erected an altar at that place called Achuzan, whence and where Enoch had been taken up to heaven

68.7 And they took sacrificial oxen and summoned all people and sacrificed the sacrifice before the Lord's face.

68.8 All people, the elders of the people and the whole assembly came to the feast and brought gifts to the sons of Enoch.

68.9 And they made a great feast, rejoicing and making merry three days, praising God, who had given them such a sign through Enoch, who had found favour with him, and that they should hand it on to their sons from generation to generation, from age to age.

68.10 Amen.

ENOCH 3

THE HEBREW
BOOK OF ENOCH

BY R. ISHMAEL BEN ELISHA
THE HIGH PRIEST

INTRODUCTION

3 ENOCH is an Old Testament Apocryphal book. 3 Enoch purports to have been written in the second century CE, but its origins can only be traced to the fifth century. Other names for 3 Enoch include "The Third Book of Enoch", "The Book of the Palaces", "The Book of Rabbi Ishmael the High Priest" and "The Revelation of Metatron".

CONTENT

Modern scholars describe this book as pseudepigraphal, as it says it is written by Rabbi Ishmael who became a 'high priest' after visions of ascension to Heaven, 90 AD - 135 AD. Rabbi Ishmael is a leading figure of Merkabah literature.

The name Sefer Hekhalot (Hekhalot meaning Palaces/Temples), along with its proposed author, places this book as a member of Hekalot/Merkabah lore. Its contents suggest that 3 Enoch's contents and ideas are newer than those shown in other Merkabah texts. The book does not contain Merkabah hymns, it has unique layout and adjuration. All these facts make 3 Enoch unique not just among Merkabah writings, but also within the writings of Enoch.

3 Enoch contains a number of Greek and Latin words. This book, unlike 1 Enoch, appears to have been originally written in Hebrew. There are a number of indications suggesting that the writers of 3 Enoch had knowledge of, and most likely read, 1 Enoch.

Some points that appear in Enoch 1 and Enoch 3 are:

Enoch ascends to Heaven in a storm chariot (3 Enoch 6:1; 7:1)

Enoch is transformed into an angel (3 Enoch 9:1-5; 15:1-2)

Enoch as an exalted angel is enthroned in Heaven (3 Enoch 10:1-3; 16:1)

Enoch receives a revelation of cosmological secrets of creation (3 Enoch 13:1-2)

The story about precious metals and how they will not avail their users and those that make idols from them (3 Enoch 5:7-14)

One of the characters is a hostile angel named Azaz'el/Aza'el (3 Enoch 4:6; 5:9)

The main themes running through 3 Enoch are the ascension of Enoch into Heaven and his transformation into the angel Metatron.

ENOCH 3

CHAPTER I

INTRODUCTION:

R. Ishmael ascends to heaven to behold the vision of the Merkaba and is given in charge to Metatron.

And Enoch walked with God: and he was not, for God took him (Gen. V. 24)

Rabbi Ishmael said:

(1) When I ascended on high to behold the vision of the Merkaba and had entered the six Halls, one within the other:

(2) as soon as I reached the door of the seventh Hall I stood still in prayer before the Holy One, blessed be He, and, lifting up my eyes on high (i.e. towards the Divine Majesty), I said:

(3) " Lord of the Universe, I pray thee, that the merit of Aaron, the son of Amram, the lover of peace and pursuer of peace, who received the crown of priesthood from Thy Glory on the mount of Sinai, be valid for me in this hour, so that Qafsiel*, the prince, and the angels with him may not get power over me nor throw me down from the heavens ".

(4) Forthwith the Holy One, blessed be He, sent to me Metatron, his Servant ('Ebed) the angel, the Prince of the Presence, and he, spreading his wings, with great joy came to meet me so as to save me from their hand.

(5) And he took me by his hand in their sight, saying to me: "Enter in peace before the high and exalted King and behold the picture of the Merkaba".

(6) Then I entered the seventh Hall, and he led me to the camp(s) of Shekina and placed me before 6the Holy One, blessed be He, to behold the Merkaba.

(7) As soon as the princes of the Merkaba and the flaming Seraphim perceived me, they fixed their eyes upon me. Instantly trembling and shuddering seized me and I fell down and was benumbed by the radiant image of their eyes and the splendid appearance of their faces; until the Holy One, blessed be He, rebuked them, saying:

(8) "My servants, my Seraphim, my Kerubim and my 'Ophanniml Cover ye your eyes before Ishmael, my son, my friend, my beloved one and my glory, that he tremble not nor shudder !"

(9) Forthwith Metatron the Prince of the Presence, came and restored my spiritand put me upon my feet.

(10) After that (moment) there was notin me strength enough to say a song before the Throne of Glory of the glorious King, the mightiest of all kings, the most excellent of all princes, until after the hour had passed.

(11) After one hour (had passed) the Holy One, blessed be He, opened to me the gates of Shekina, the gates of Peace, the gates of Wisdom, the gates of Strength, the gates of Power, the gates of Speech (Dibbur), the gates of

Song, the gates of Qedushsha, the gates of Chant.

(12) And he enlightened my eyes and my heart by words of psalm, song, praise, exaltation, thanksgiving, extolment, glorification, hymn and eulogy. And as I opened my mouth, uttering a song before the Holy One, blessed be He, the Holy Chayyoth beneath and above the Throne of Glory answered and said: "HOLY " and "BLESSED BE THE GLORY OF YHWH FROM HIS PLACE !"

(i.e. chanted the Qedushsha).

CHAPTER II

The highest classes of angels make inquiries about R. Ishmael which are answered by Metatron

R. Ishmael said:

(1) In that hour the eagles of the Merkaba, the flaming 'Ophannim and the Seraphim of consuming fire asked Metatron, saying to him:

(2) "Youth ! Why sufferest thou one born of woman to enter and behold the Merkaba? From which nation, from which tribe is this one? What is his character?"

(3) Metatron answered and said to them: "From the nation of Israel whom the Holy One, blessed be He, chose for his people from among seventy tongues (nations), from the tribe of Levi, whom he set aside as a contribution to his name and from the seed of Aaron whom the Holy One, blessed be He, did choose for his servant and put upon him the crown of priesthood on Sinai".

(4) Forthwith they spake and said: "Indeed, this one is worthy to behold the Merkaba ". And they said: "Happy is the people that is in such a case!".

CHAPTER III

Metatron has 70 names, but God calls him 'Youth'

R. Ishmael said:

(1) In that hour1 I asked Metatron, the angel, the Prince of the Presence: "What is thy name?"

(2) He answered me: "I have seventy names, corresponding to the seventy tongues of the world and all of them are based upon the name Metatron, angel of the Presence; but my King calls me 'Youth' (Na'ar)"

CHAPTER IV

Metatron is identical with Enoch who was translated to heaven at the time of the Deluge

R. Ishmael said:

(1) I asked Metatron and said to him: "Why art thou called by the name of thy Creator, by seventy names? Thou art greater than all the princes, higher than all the angels, beloved more than all the servants, honoured above all the mighty ones in kingship, greatness and glory: why do they call thee ' Youth ' in the high heavens ?"

(2) He answered and said to me: " Because I am Enoch, the son of Jared.

(3) For when the generation of the flood sinned and were confounded in their deeds, saying unto God: 'Depart from us, for we desire not the knowledge of thy ways' (Job xxi. 14), then the Holy One, blessed be He, removed me from their midst to be a witness against them in the high heavens to all the inhabitants of the world, that they may not say: 'The Merciful One is cruel".

(4) What sinned all those multitudes, their wives, their sons and their, daughters, their horses, their mules and their cattle and their property, and all the birds of the world, all of which the Holy One, blessed be He, destroyed from the world together with them in the waters of the flood?

(5) Hence the Holy One, blessed be He, lifted me up in their lifetime before their eyes to be a witness against them to the future world. And the Holy One, blessed be He, assigned me for a prince and a ruler among the ministering angels.

(6) In that hour three of the ministering angels, 'UZZA, 'AZZA and 'AZZAEL came forth and brought charges against me in the high heavens, saying before the Holy One, blessed be He: "Said not the Ancient Ones (First Ones) rightly before Thee: < Do not create man! ' " The Holy One, blessed be He, answered and said unto them: "I have made and I will bear, yea, I will carry and will deliver". (Is. xlvi. 4.)

(7) As soon as they saw me, they said before Him: "Lord of the Universe ! What is this one that he should ascend to the height of heights? Is not he one from among the sons of [the sons of] those who perished in the days of the Flood? "What doeth he in the Raqia'?"

(8) Again, the Holy One, blessed be He, answered and said to them: "What are ye, that ye enter and speak in my presence? I delight in this one more than in all of you, and hence he shall be a prince and a ruler over you in the high heavens."

(9) Forthwith all stood up and went out to meet me, prostrated themselves before me and said: "Happy art thou and happy is thy father for thy Creator doth favour thee".

(10) And because I am small and a youth among them in days, months and years, therefore they call me "Youth" (Na'ar).

CHAPTER V

The idolatry of the generation of Enosh causes God to remove the Shekina from earth. The idolatry inspired by 'Azza, 'Uzza and 'Azziel

R.Ishmael said: Metatron, the Prince of the Presence, said to me:

(1) From the day when the Holy One, blessed be He, expelled the first Adam from the Garden of Eden (and onwards), Shekina was dwelling upon a Kerub under the Tree of Life.

(2) And the ministering angels were gathering together and going down from heaven in parties, from the Raqia in companies and from the heavens in camps to do His will in the whole world.

(3) And the first man and his generation were sitting outside the gate of the Garden to behold the radiant appearance of the Shekina.

(4) For the silendour of the Shekina traversed the world from one end to the other (with a splendour) 365,000 times (that) of the globe of the sun. And everyone who made use of the splendour of the Shekina, on him no flies and no gnats did rest, neither was he ill nor suffered he any pain. No demons got power over him, neither were they able to injure him.

(5) When the Holy One, blessed be He, went out and went in: from the Garden to Eden, from Eden to the Garden, from the Garden to Raqia and from Raqia to the Garden of Eden then all and everyone beheld the splendour of His Shekina and they were not injured;

(6) until uthe time of the generation of Enosh who was the head of all idol worshippers of the world.

(7) And what did the generation of Enosh do? They went from one end of the world to the other, and each one brought silver, gold, precious stones and pearls in heaps like unto mountains and hills making idols out of them throughout all the world. And they erected the idols in every quarter of the world: the size of each idol was 1000 parasangs.

(8) And they brought down the sun, the moon, planets and constellations, and placed them before the idols on their right hand and on their left, to attend them even as they attend the Holy One, blessed be He, as it is written (1 Kings xxii. 19): "And all the host of heaven was standing by him on his right hand and on his left".

(9) What power was in them that they were able to bring them down? They would not have been able to bring them down but for 'Uzza, 'Azza and 'Azziel who taught them sorceries whereby they brought them down and made use of them

(10) In that time the ministering angels brought charges (against them) before the Holy One, blessed be He, saying before him: "Master of the World! What hast thou to do with the children of men? As it is written (Ps. viii. 4) 'What is man (Enosh) that thou art mindful of him?' 'Mah Adam' is not written here, but 'Mah Enosh', for he (Enosh) is the head of the idol worshippers.

(11) Why hast thou left the highest of the high heavens, the abode of thy glorious Name, and the high and exalted Throne in 'Araboth Raqia' in the highest and art gone and dwellest with the children of men who worship idols and equal thee to the idols.

(12) Now thou art on earth and the idols likewise. What hast thou to do with the inhabitants of the earth who worship idols?"

(13) Forthwith the Holy One, blessed be He, lifted up His Shekina from the earth, from their midst.

(14) In that moment came the ministering angels, the troops of hosts and the armies of 'Araboth in thousand camps and ten thousand hosts: they fetched trumpets and took the horns in their hands and surrounded the Shekina with all kinds of songs.And He ascended to the high heavens, as it is written (Ps. xlvii. **5**): "God is gone up with a shout, the Lord with the sound of a trumpet ".

CHAPTER VI

Enoch lifted up to heaven together with the Shekina. Angels protests answered by God

R. Ishmael said: Metatron, the Angel, the Prince of the Presence, said to me:

(1) When the Holy One, blessed be He, desired to lift me up on high, He first sent 'Anaphiel H (H = Tetragrammaton) the Prince, and he took me from their midst in their sight and carried me in great glory upon a a fiery chariot with fiery horses, servants of glory. And he lifted me up to the high heavens together with the Shekina.

(2) As soon as I reached the high heavens, the Holy Chayyoth, the 'Ophannim, the Seraphim, the Kerubim, the Wheels of the Merkaba (the Galgallim), and the ministers of the consuming fire, perceiving my smell from a distance of 365,000 myriads of parasangs, said: "What smell of one born of woman and what taste of a white drop (is this) that ascends on high, and (lo, he is merely) a gnat among those who 'divide flames (of fire)'?"

(3) The Holy One, blessed be He, answered and spake unto them: "My servants, my hosts, my Kerubim, my 'Ophannim, my Seraphim! Be ye not displeased on account of this! Since all the children of men have denied me and my great Kingdom and are gone worshipping idols, I have removed my Shekina from among them and have

lifted it up on high. But this one whom I have taken from among them is an ELECT ONE among (the inhabitants of) the world and he is equal to all of them in faith, righteousness and perfection of deed and I have taken him for (as) a tribute from my world under all the heavens".

CHAPTER VII

Enoch raised upon the wings of the Shekina to the place of the Throne, the Merkaba and the angelic hosts

R. Ishmael said: Metatron, the Angel, the Prince of the Presence, said to me:

(1) When the Holy One, blessed be He, took me away from the generation of the Flood, he lifted me on the wings of the wind of Shekina to the highest heaven and brought me into the great palaces of the 'Araboth Raqia' on high, where are the glorious Throne of Shekina, the Merkaba, the troops of anger, the armies of vehemence, the fiery Shin'anim', the flaming Kerubim, and the burning 'Ophannim, the flaming servants, the flashing Chashmattim and the lightening Seraphim. And he placed me (there) to attend the Throne of Glory day after day.

CHAPTER VIII

The gates (of the treasuries of heaven) opened to Metatron

R. Ishmael said: Metatron, the Prince of the Presence, said to me:

(1) Before He appointed me to attend the Throne of Glory, the Holy One, blessed be He, opened to me three

hundred thousand gates of Under-standing three hundred thousand gates of Subtlety three hundred thousand gates of Life three hundred thousand gates of grace and loving-kindness three hundred thousand gates of love three hundred thousand gates of Tora three hundred thousand gates of meek-ness three hundred thousand gates of maintenance three hundred thousand gates' of mercy three hundred thou-sand gates of fear of heaven

(2) In that hour the Holy One, blessed be He, added in me wisdom unto wis-dom, understanding unto understand-ing, subtlety unto subtlety, knowledge unto knowledge, mercy unto mercy, instruction unto instruction, love unto love, loving-kindness unto loving-kindness, goodness unto goodness, meekness unto meekness, power unto power, strength unto strength, might unto might, brilliance unto brilliance, beauty unto beauty, splendour unto splendour, and I was honoured and adorned with all these good and praiseworthy things more than all the children of heaven.

CHAPTER IX

Enoch receives blessings from the Most High and is adorned with an-gelic attributes

R. Ishmael said: Metatron, the Prince of the Presence, said to me:

(1) After all these things the Holy One, blessed be He, put His hand upon me and blessed me with 536 O bless-ings.

(2) And I was raised and enlarged to the size of the length and width of the world.

(3) And He caused 72 wings to grow on me, 36 on each side. And each wing was as the whole world.

(4) And He fixed on me 365 eyes: each eye was as the great luminary.

(5) And He left no kind of splendour, brilliance, radiance, beauty in (of) all the lights of the universe that He did not fix on me.

CHAPTER X

God places Metatron on a throne at the door of the seventh Hall and announces through the Herald, that Metatron henceforth is God's representative and ruler over all the princes of kingdoms and all the children of heaven, save the eight high princes called YHWH by the name of their King

R. Ishmael said: Metatron, the Prince of the Presence, said to me:

(1) All these things the Holy One, blessed be He, made for me:He made me a Throne, similar to the Throne of Glory. And He spread over me a cur-tain of splendour and brilliant appearance, of beauty, grace and mercy, similar to the curtain of the Throne of Glory; and on it were fixed all kinds of lights in the universe.

(2) And He placed it at the door of the Seventh Hall and seated me on it.

(3) And the herald went forth into every heaven, saying:This is Meta-tron, my servant. I have made him into a prince and a ruler over all the princes of my kingdoms and over all the children of heaven, except the eight great princes, the honoured and revered ones who are called YHWH, by the name of their King.

(4) And every angel and every prince who has a word to speak in my presence (before me) shall go into his presence (before him) and shall speak to him (instead).

(5) And every command that he utters to you in my name do ye observe and fulfil. For the Prince of Wisdom and the Prince of Understanding have I committed to him to instruct him in the wisdom of heavenly things and of earthly things, in the wisdom of this world and of the world to come.

(6) Moreover, I have set him over all the treasuries of the palapes of Araboih and over all the stores of life that I have in the high heavens.

CHAPTER XI

God reveals all mysteries and secrets to Metatron

R. Ishmael said: Metatron, the angel, the Prince of the Presence, said to me:

(1) Henceforth the Holy One, blessed be He, revealed to me all the mysteries of Tora and all the secrets of wisdom and all the depths of the Perfect Law; and all living beings' thoughts of heart and all the secrets of the universe and all the secrets of Creation were revealed unto me even as they are revealed unto the Maker of Creation.

(2) And I watched intently to behold the secrets of the depth and the wonderful mystery. Before a man did think in secret, I saw (it) and before a man made a thing I beheld it.

(3) And there was no thing on high nor in the deep hidden from me.

CHAPTER XII

God clothes Metatron in a garment of glory, puts a royalcrown on his head and calls him "the Lesser YHWH"

R. Ishmael said: Metatron, the Prince of the Presence, said to me:

(1) By reason of the love with which the Holy One, blessed be He, loved me more than all the children of heaven, He made me a garment of glory on which were fixed all kinds of lights, and He clad me in it.

(2) And He made me a robe of honour on which were fixed all kinds of beauty, splendour, brilliance and majesty.

(3) And he made me a royal crown in which were fixed forty-nine costly stones like unto the light of the globe of the sun.

(4) For its splendour went forth in the four quarters of the 'Araboth Raqia', and in (through) the seven heavens, and in the four quarters of the world. And he put it on my head.

(5) And He called me THE LESSER YHWH in the presence of all His heavenly household; as it is written (Ex. xxiii. 21): "For my name is in him".

CHAPTER XIII

God writes with a flaming style on Metatron's crown the cosmic letters by which heaven and earth were created

R. Ishmael said: Metatron, the angel, the Prince of the Presence, the Glory of all heavens, said to me:

(1) Because of the great love and mercy with which the Holy One, blessed be He, loved and cherished me more than all the children of heaven, He wrote with his ringer with a flaming style upon the crown on my head the letters by which were created heaven and earth, the seas and rivers, the mountains and hills, the planets and constellations, the lightnings, winds, earthquakes and voices (thunders), the snow and hail, the stormwind and the tempest ; the letters by which were created all the needs of the world and all the orders of Creation.

(2) And every single letter sent forth time after time as it were lightnings, time after time as it were torches, time after time as it were flames of fire, time after time (rays) like [as] the rising of the sun and the moon and the planets.

CHAPTER XIV

All the highest princes, the elementary angels and the planetary and sideric angels fear and tremble at the sight of Metatron crowned

R. Ishmael said: Metatron, the Angel, the Prince of the Presence, said to me:

(1) When the Holy One, blessed be He, put this crown on my head, (then) trembled before me all the Princes of Kingdoms who are in the height of 'Araboth Raqiaf and all the hosts of every heaven; and even the princes (of) the 'Elim, the princes (of) the 'Er'ellim and the princes (of) the Tafsarim, who are greater than all the ministering angels who minister before the Throne of Glory, shook, feared and trembled before me when they beheld me.

(2) Even Sammael, the Prince of the Accusers, who is greater than all the princes of kingdoms on high; feared and trembled before me.

(3) And even the angel of fire, and the angel of hail, and the angel of the wind, and the angel of the lightning, and the angel of anger, and the angel of the thunder, and the angel of the snow, and the angel of the rain ; and the angel of the day, and the angel of the night, and the angel of the sun and the angel of the moon, and the angel of the planets and the angel of the constellations who rule the world under their hands, feared and trembled and were affrighted before me, when they beheld me.

(4) These are the names of the rulers of the world: Gabriel, the angel of the fire, Baradiel, the angel of the hail, Ruchiel who is appointed over the wind, Baraqiel who is appointed over the lightnings, Za'amiel who is appointed over the vehemence, Ziqiel who is appointed over the sparks, Zi'iel who is appointed over the commotion, Zdaphiel who is appointed over the storm-wind, Ra'amiel who is

appointed over the thunders, Rctashiel who is appointed over the earthquake, Shalgiel who is appointed over the snow, Matariel who is appointed over the rain, Shimshiel who is appointed over the day, Lailiel who is appointed over the night, Galgalliel who is appointed over the globe of the sun, 'Ophanniel who is appointed over the globe of the moon, Kokbiel who is appointed over the planets, Rahatiel who is appointed over the constellations.

(5) And they all fell prostrate, when they saw me. And they were not able to behold me because of the majestic glory and beauty of the appearance of the shining light of the crown of glory upon my head.

CHAPTER XV

Metatron transformed into fire

R. Ishmael said: Metatron, the angel, the Prince of the Presence, the Glory of all heavens, said to me:

(1) As soon as the Holy One, blessed be He, took me in (His) service to attend the Throne of Glory and the Wheels (Galgallim) of the Merkaba and the needs of Shekina, forthwith my flesh was changed into flames, my sinews into flaming fire, my bones into coals of burning juniper, the light of my eyelids into splendour of lightnings, my eyeballs into fire-brands, the hair of my head into dot flames, all my limbs into wings of burning fire and the whole of my body into glowing fire.

(2) And on my right were divisions 6 of fiery flames, on my left fire-brands

were burning, round about me storm-wind and tempest were blowing and in front of me and behind me was roaring of thunder with earthquake.

FRAGMENT OF 'ASCENSION OF MOSES'

(1) R. Ishmael said: Said to me Metatron, the Prince of the Presence and the prince over all the princes and he stands befote Him who is greater than all the Elohim. And he goes in under the Throne of Glory. And he has a great tabernacle of light on high. And he brings forth the fire of deafness and puts (it) into the ears of the Holy Chayyoth, that they may not hear the voice of the Word (Dibbur) that goes forth from the mouth of the Divine Majesty.

(2) And when Moses ascended on high, he fasted 121 fasts, till the habitations of the chashmal were opened to him; and he saw the heart within the heart of the Lion and he saw the innumerable companies of the hosts Around about him. And they desired to burn him. But Moses prayed for mercy, first for Israel and after that for himself: and He who sitteth on the Merkaba opened the windows that are above the heads of the Kerubim. And a host of 1800 advocates and the Prince of the Presence, Metatron, with them went forth to meet Moses. And they took the prayers of Israel and put them as a crown on the head of the Holy One, blessed be He.

(3) And they said (Deut. vi. 4): "Hear, O Israel; the Lord our God is one Lord"and their face shone and rejoiced over Shekinaand they said to Metatron: "What are these? And to

whom do they give all this honour and glory?" And they answered: "To the Glorious Lord of Israel". And they spake: "Hear, O Israel: the Lord, our God, is one Lord. To whom shall be given abundance of honour and majesty but to Thee YHWH, the Divine Majesty, the King, living and eternal".

(4) In that moment spake Akatriel Yah Yehod Sebaoth and said to Metatron, the Prince of the Presence: "Let no prayer that he prayeth before me return (to him) void. Hear thou his prayer and fulfil his desire whether (it be) great or small".

(5) Forthwith Metatron, the Prince of the Presence, said to Moses:

"Son of Amram! Fear not, for now God delights in thee. And ask thou u thy desire of the Glory and Majesty. For thy face shines from one end of the world to the other". But Moses answered him: "(I fear) lest I bring guiltiness upon myself". Metatron said to him: "Receive the letters of the oath, in (by) which there is no breaking the covenant" (which precludes any breach of the covenant).

CHAPTER XVI

1 Probably additional

Metatron divested of his privilege of presiding on a Throne of his own on account of Acher's misapprehension in taking him for a second Divine Power

R. Ishmael said: Metatron, the Angel, the Prince of the Presence, the Glory of all heaven, said to me:

(1) At first I was sitting upon a great Throne at the door of the Seventh Hall ; and I was judging the children of heaven, the household on high by authority of the Holy One, blessed be He. And I divided Greatness, Kingship, Dignity, Rulership, Honour and Praise, and Diadem and Crown of Glory unto all the princes of kingdoms, while I was presiding (lit. sitting) in the Celestial Court (Yeshiba), and the princes of kingdoms were standing before me, on my right and on my left by authority of the Holy One, blessed be He.

(2) But when Acher came to behold the vision of the Merkaba and fixed his eyes on me, he feared and trembled before me and his soul was affrighted even unto departing from him, because of fear, horror and dread of me, when he beheld me sitting upon a throne like a king with all the ministering angels standing by me as my servants and all the princes of kingdoms adorned with crowns surrounding me:

(3) in that moment he opened his mouth and said: "Indeed, there are two Divine Powers in heaven!" **(4)** Forthwith Bath Qol (the Divine Voice) went forth from heaven from before the Shekina and said: "Return, ye backsliding children (Jer. iii. 22), except Acher!"

(5) Then came 'Aniyel, the Prince, the honoured, glorified, beloved, wonderful, revered and fearful one, in commission from the Holy One, blessed be He and gave me sixty strokes with lashes of fire and made me stand on my feet.

CHAPTER XVII

The princes of the seven heavens, of the sun, moon, planets and constellations and their suites of angels

R. Ishmael said: Metatron, the angel, the Prince of the Presence, the glory of all heavens, said to me:

(1) Seven (are the) princes, the great, beautiful, revered, wonderful and honoured ones who are appointed over the seven heavens. And these are they: MIKAEL, GABRIEL, SHATQIEL, SHACHAQIEL, BAKARIEL, BADARIEL, PACHRIEL.

(2) And every one of them is the prince of the host of (one) heaven. And each one of them is accompanied by 496,000 myriads of ministering angels.

(3) MIKAEL, the great prince, is appointed over the seventh heaven, the highest one, which is in the 'Araboth. GABRIEL, the prince of the host, is appointed over the sixth heaven which is in Makon.

SHATAQIEL, prince of the host, is appointed over the fifth heaven which is in Ma'on.

SHAHAQi'EL, prince of the host, is appointed over the fourth heaven which is in Zebul.

BADARIEL, prince of the host, is appointed over the third heaven which is in Shehaqim. BARAKIEL, prince of the host, is appointed over the second heaven which is in the height of (Merom) Raqia.

PAZRIEL, prince of the host, is appointed over the first heaven which is in Wilon, which is in Shamayim.

(4) Under them is GALGALLIEL, the prince who is appointed over the globe (galgal) of the sun, and with him are 96 great and honoured angels who move the sun in Raqia'.

(5) Under them is 'OPHANNIEL, the prince who is set over the globe ('ophari) of the moon. And with him are 88 angels who move the globe of the moon 354 thousand parasangs every night at the time when the moon stands in the East at its turning point. And when is the moon sitting in the East at its turning point? Answer: in the fifteenth day of every month.

(6) Under them is RAHATIEL, the prince who is appointed over the constellations. And he is accompanied by 72 great and honoured angels. And why is he called RAHATIEL? Because he makes the stars run (marhit) in their orbits and courses 339 thousand parasangs every night from the East to the West, and from the West to the East. For the Holy One, blessed be He, has made a tent for all of them, for the sun, the moon, the planets and the stars in which they travel at night from the West to the East.

(7) Under them is KOKBIEL, the prince who is appointed over all the planets. And with him are 365,000 myriads of ministering angels, great and honoured ones who move the planets from city to city and from province to province in the Raqia' of heavens.

(8) And over them are SEVENTY-TWO PRINCES OF KINGDOMS on high corresponding to the 72 tongues of the world. And all of them are crowned with royal crowns and clad in royal garments and wrapped in royal cloaks. And all of them are riding on royal horses and they are holding royal sceptres in their hands. And before each one of them when he is travelling in Raqia', royal servants are running with great glory and majesty even as on earth they (princes) are travelling in chariot(s) with horsemen and great armies and in glory and greatness with praise, song and honour.

CHAPTER XVIII

The order of ranks of the angels and the homage received by the higher ranks from the lower ones

R. Ishmael said: Metatron, the Angel, the Prince of the Presence, the glory of all heaven, said to me:

(1) THE ANGELS OF THE FIRST HEAVEN, when(ever) they see their prince, they dismount from their horses and fall on their faces.

And THE PRINCE OF THE FIRST HEAVEN, when he sees the prince of the second heaven, he dismounts, removes the crown of glory from his head and falls on his face.

And THE PRINCE OF THE SECOND HEAVEN, when he sees the Prince of the third heaven, he removes the crown of glory from his head and falls on his face.

And THE PRINCE OF THE THIRD HEAVEN, when he sees the prince of the fourth heaven, he removes the crown of glory from his head and falls on his face.

And THE PRINCE OF THE FOURTH HEAVEN, when he sees the prince of the fifth heaven, he removes the crown of glory from his head and falls on his face.

And THE PRINCE OF THE FIFTH HEAVEN, when he sees the prince of the sixth heaven, he removes the crown of glory from his head and falls on his face.

And THE PRINCE OF THE SIXTH HEAVEN, when he sees the prince of the seventh heaven, he removes the crown of glory from his head and falls on his face.

(2) And THE PRINCE OF THE SEVENTH HEAVEN, when he sees THE SEVENTYTWO PRINCES OF KINGDOMS, he removes the crown of glory from his head and falls on his face.

(3) And the seventy-two princes of kingdoms, when they see THE DOOR KEEPERS OF THE FIRST HALL IN THE ARABOTH RAQIA in the highest, they remove the royal crown from their head and fall on their faces.

And THE DOOR KEEPERS OF THE FIRST HALL, when they see the door keepers of the second Hall, they remove the crown of glory from their head and fall on their faces.

And THE DOOR KEEPERS OF THE SECOND HALL, when they see the door keepers of the third Hall, they remove the crown of glory from their head and fall on their faces.

And THE DOOR KEEPERS OF THE THIRD HALL, when they see the door keepers of the fourth Hall, they remove the crown of glory from their head and fall on their faces.

And THE DOOR KEEPERS OF THE FOURTH HALL, when they see the door keepers of the fifth Hall, they remove the crown of glory from their head and fall on their faces.

And THE DOOR KEEPERS OF THE FIFTH HALL, when they see the door keepers of the sixth Hall, they remove the crown of glory from their head and fall on their faces.

And THE DOOR KEEPERS OF THE SIXTH HALL, when they see the DOOR KEEPERS OF THE SEVENTH HALL, they remove the crown of glory from their head and fall on their faces.

(4) And the door keepers of the seventh Hall, when they see THE FOUR GREAT PRINCES, the honoured ones, WHO ARE APPOINTED OVER THE FOUR CAMPS OF SHEKINA, they remove the crown(s) of glory from their head and fall on their faces.

(5) And the four great princes, when they see TAG'AS, the prince, great and honoured with song (and) praise, at the head of all thechildren of heaven, they remove the crown of glory from their head and fall on their faces.

(6) And Tag' as, the great and honoured prince, when he sees BARATTIEL, the great prince of three fingers in the height of 'Araboth, the highest heaven, he removes the crown of glory from his head and falls on his face.

(7) And Barattiel, the great prince, when he sees HAMON, the great prince, the fearful and honoured, pleasant and terrible one who maketh all the children of heaven to tremble, when the time draweth nigh (that is set) for the saying of the '(Thrice) Holy', as it is written (Isa. xxxiii. 3): "At the noise of the tumult (hamon) the peoples are fled; at the lifting up of thyself the nations are scattered" he removes the crown of glory from his head and falls on his face.

(8) And Hamon, the great prince, when he sees TUTRESIEL, the great prince, he removes the crown of glory from his head and falls on his face.

(9) And Tutresiel H', the great prince, when he sees ATRUGIEL, the great prince, he removes the crown of glory from his head and falls on his face.

(10) And Atrugiel the great prince, when he sees NA'ARIRIEL H', the great prince, he removes the crown of glory from his head and falls on his face.

(11) And Na'aririel H', the great prince, when he sees SASNIGIEL H', the great prince, he removes the crown of glory from his head and falls on his face.

(12) And Sasnigiel H', when he sees ZAZRIEL H', the great prince, he removes the crown of glory from his head and falls on his face.

(13) And Zazriel H', the prince, when he sees GEBURATIEL H', the prince,

he removes the crown of glory from his head and falls on his face.

(14) And Geburatiel H', the prince, when he sees 'ARAPHIEL H', the prince, he removes the crown of glory from his head and falls on his face.

(15) And 'Araphiel H', the prince, when he sees 'ASHRUYLU, the prince, who presides in all the sessions of the children of heaven, he removes the crown of glory from his head and falls on his face.

(16) And Ashruylu H, the prince, when he sees GALLISUR H', THE PRINCE, WHO REVEALS ALL THE SECRETS OF THE LAW (Tora), he removes the crown of glory from his head and falls on his face.

(17) And Gallisur H', the prince, when he sees ZAKZAKIEL H', the prince who is appointed to write down the merits of Israel on the Throne of Glory, he removes the crown of glory from his head and falls on his face.

(18) And Zakzakiel H', the great prince, when he sees 'ANAPHIEL H', the prince who keeps the keys of the heavenly Halls, he removes the crown of glory from his head and falls on his face. Why is he called by the name of 'Anaphiel ? Because the bough of his honour and majesty and his crown and his splendour and his brilliance covers (overshadows) all the chambers of 'Araboth Raqia on high even as the Maker of the World (doth overshadow them). Just as it is written with regard to the Maker of the World (Hab. iii. **3**): "His glory covered the heavens, and the earth was full of his praise", even so do the honour and majesty of 'Anaphiel cover all the glories of 'Araboth the highest.

(19) And when he sees SOTHER 'ASHIEL H', the prince, the great, fearful and honoured one, he removes the crown of glory from his head and falls on his face. Why is he called Sother Ashiel? Because he is appointed over the four heads of the fiery river over against the Throne of Glory; and every single prince who goes out or enters before the Shekina, goes out or enters only by his permission.

For the seals of the fiery river are entrusted to him. And furthermore, his height is 7000 myriads of parasangs. And he stirs up the fire of the river ; and he goes out and enters before the Shekina to expound what is written (recorded) concerning the inhabitants of the world. According as it is written (Dan. vii. 10): "the judgement was set, and the books were opened".

(20) And Sother 'Ashiel the prince, when he sees SHOQED CHOZI, the great prince, the mighty, terrible and honoured one, he removes the crown of glory from his head and falls upon his face.

And why is he called Shoqed Chozi?

Because he weighs all the merits (of man) in a balance in the presence of the Holy One, blessed be He.

(21) And when he sees ZEHANPURYUH', the great prince, the mighty and terrible one, honoured, glorified and feared in all the heavenly household, he removes the crown of glory from his head and falls on his face. Why is he called Zehanpuryu?

Because he rebukes the fiery river and pushes it back to its place.

(22) And when he sees 'AZBUGA H', the great prince, glorified, revered, honoured, adorned, wonderful, exalted, beloved and feared among all the great princes who know the mystery of the Throne of Glory, he removes the crown of glory from his head and falls on his face. Why is he called 'Azbuga? Because in the future he will gird (clothe) the righteous and pious of the world with the garments of life and wrap them in the cloak of life, that they may live in them an eternal life.

(23) And when he sees the two great princes, the strong and glorified ones who are standing above him, he removes the crown of glory from his head and falls on his face. And these are the names of the two princes:

SOPHERIEL H' (WHO) KILLETH,

(Sopheriel H' the Killer), the great prince, the honoured, glorified, blameless, venerable, ancient and mighty one; (and) SOPHERIEL H' (WHO) MAKETH ALIVE

(Sopheriel H' the Lifegiver), the great prince, the honoured, glorified, blameless, ancient and mighty one.

(24) Why is he called Sopheriel H' who killeth (Sopheriel H' the Killer)? Because he is appointed over the books of the dead: [so that] everyone, when the day of his death draws nigh, he writes him in the books of the dead.

Why is he called Sopheriel H' who maketh alive (Sopheriel H' the Lifegiver)? Because he is appointed over the books of the living (of life),

so that every one whom the Holy One, blessed be He, will bring into life, he writes him in the book of the living (of life), by authority of MAQOM. Thou might perhaps say: "Since the Holy One, blessed be He, is sitting on a throne, they also are sitting when writing". (Answer): The Scripture teaches us (1 Kings xxii. 19, 2 Chron. xviii. 18): "And all the host of heaven are standing by him ".

"The host of heaven " (it is said) in order to show us, that even the Great Princes, none like whom there is in the high heavens, do not fulfil the requests of the Shekina otherwise than standing. But how is it (possible that) they (are able to) write, when they are standing?

It is like this:

(25) One is standing on the wheels of the tempest and the other is standing on the wheels of the storm-wind. The one is clad in kingly garments, the other is clad in kingly garments.

The one is wrapped in a mantle of majesty and the other is wrapped in a mantle of majesty.

The one is crowned with a royal crown, and the other is crowned with a royal crown. The one's body is full of eyes, and the other's body is full of eyes.

The appearance of one is like unto the appearance of lightnings, and the appearance of the other is like unto the appearance of lightnings.

The eyes of the one are like the sun in its might, and the eyes of the other are like the sun in its might.

The one's height is like the height of the seven heavens, and the other's height is like the height of the seven heavens.

The wings of the one are as (many as) the days of the year, and the wings of the other are as (many as) the days of the year.

The wings of the one extend over the breadth of Raqia', and the wings of the other extend over the breadth of Ra-qia. The lips of the one, are as the gates of the East, and the lips of the other are as the gates of the East.

The tongue of the one is as high as the waves of the sea, and the tongue of the other is as high as the waves of the sea.

From the mouth of the one a flame goes forth, and from the mouth of the other a flame goes forth.

From the mouth of the one there go forth lightnings and from the mouth of the other there go forth lightnings.

From the sweat of the one fire is kindled, and from the perspiration of the other fire is kindled.

From the one's tongue a torch is burning, and from the tongue of the other a torch is burning.

On the head of the one there is a sapphire stone, and upon the head of the other there is a sapphire stone.

On the shoulders of the one there is a wheel of a swift cherub, and on the shoulders of the other there is a wheel of a swift cherub. One has in his hand a burning scroll, the other has in his hand a burning scroll. The one has in his hand a flaming style, the other has in his hand a flaming style. The length of the scroll is **3000** myriads of para-sangs ; the size of the style is **3OOO** myriads of parasangs; the size of every single letter that they write is **365** parasangs.

CHAPTER XIX

Rikbiel, the prince of the wheels of the Merkaba. The surroundings of the Merkaba. The commotion among the angelic hosts at the time of the Qedushsha

R. Ishmael said: Metatron, the Angel, the Prince of the Presence, said to me:

(1) Above **2** these three angels, these great princes there is one Prince, distinguished, honoured, noble, glorified, adorned, fearful, valiant, strong, great, magnified, glorious, crowned, wonderful, exalted, blameless, beloved, lordly, high and lofty, ancient and mighty, like unto whom there is none among the princes. His name is RIKBIEL H', the great and revered Prince who is standing by the Merkaba.

(2) And why is he called RIKBIEL?

Because he is appointed over the wheels of the Merkaba, and they are given in his charge.

(3) And how many are the wheels? Eight; two in each direction. And there are four winds compassing them round about. And these are their names: "the Storm-Wind", "the Tempest", "the Strong Wind", and "the Wind of Earthquake".

(4) And under them four fieryrivers are continually running, one fiery river on each side. And round about them, between the rivers, four clouds are planted (placed), and these they are: "clouds of fire", "clouds of lamps", "clouds of coal", "clouds of brimstone" and they are standing over against [their] wheels.

(5) And the feet of the Chayyoth are resting upon the wheels. And between one wheel and the other earthquake is roaring and thunder is thundering.

(6) And when the time draws nigh for the recital of the Song, (then) the multitudes of wheels are moved, the multitude of clouds tremble, all the chieftains (shallishim) are made afraid, all the horsemen (parashim) do rage, all the mighty ones (gibborim) are excited, all the hosts (seba'im) are afrighted, all the troops (gedudim) are in fear, all the appointed ones (memunnim) haste away, all the princes (sarim) and armies (chayyelim) are dismayed, all the servants (mesharetim) do faint and all the angels (mal'akim) and divisions (degalim) travail with pain.

(7) And one wheel makes a sound to be heard to the other and one Kerub to another, one Chayya. to another, one Seraph to another (saying) (Ps. lxviii. 5) "Extol to him that rideth in 'Araboth, by his name Jah and rejoice before him!"

CHAPTER XX

CHAYYLIEL, the prince of the Chayyoth

R. Ishmael said: Metatron, the angel, the Prince of the Presence, said to me:

(1) Above these there is one great and mighty prince. His name is CHAYYLIEL H', a noble and revered prince, a glorious and mighty prince, a great and revered prince, a prince before whom all the children of heaven do tremble, a prince who is able to swallow up the whole earth in one moment (at a mouthful).

(2) And why is he called CHAYYLIEL H'? Because he is appointed over the Holy Chayyoth and smites the Chayyoth with lashes of fire: and glorifies them, when they give praise and glory and rejoicing and he causes them to make haste to say "Holy" and "Blessed be the Glory of H' from his place!" (i.e. the Qedushshd).

CHAPTER XXI

The Chayyoth

R. Ishmael said: Metatron, the angel, the Prince of the Presence, said to me:

(1) Four (are) the Chayyoth corresponding to the four winds. Each Chayya is as the space of the whole world. And each one has four faces ; and each face is as the face of the East.

(2) Each one has four wings and each wing is like the cover (roof) of the universe.

(3) And each one has faces in the middle of faces and wings in the middle of wings. The size of the faces is (as the size of) 248 faces, and the size of the wings is (as the size of) 365 wings.

(4) And every one is crowned with 2000 crowns on his head. And each crown is like unto the bow in the cloud. And its splendour is like unto the splendour of the globe of the sun. And the sparks that go forth from every one are like the splendour of the morning star (planet Venus) in the East.

CHAPTER XXII a

KERUBIEL, the Prince of the Kerubim. Description of the Kerubim

R. Ishmael said: Metatron, the angel, the Prince of the Presence, said to me:

(1) Above these la there is one prince, noble, wonderful, strong, and praised with all kinds of praise. His name is KERUBIEL H', a mighty prince, full of power and strength a prince of highness, and Highness (is) with him, a righteous prince, and righteousness (is) with him, a holy prince, and holiness (is) with him, a prince glorified in (by) thousand hosts, exalted by ten thousand armies.

(2) At his wrath the earth trembles, at his anger the camps are moved, from fear of him the foundations are shaken, at his rebuke the 'Araboth do tremble.

(3) His stature is full of (burning) coals. The height of his stature is as the height of the seven heavens the breadth of his stature is as the wideness of the seven heavens and the thickness of his stature is as the seven heavens.

(4) The opening of his mouth is like a lamp of fire. His tongue is a consuming fire. His eyebrows are like unto the splendour of the lightning. His eyes are like sparks of brilliance. His countenance is like a burning fire.

(5) And there is a crown of holiness upon his head on which (crown) the Explicit Name is graven, and lightnings go forth from it. And the bow of Shekina is between his shoulders.

(6) And his sword is like unto a lightning; and upon his loins there are arrows like unto a flame, and upon his armour and shield there is a consuming fire, and upon his neck there are coals of burning juniper and (also) round about him (there are coals of burning juniper).

(7) And the splendour of Shekina is on his face ; and the horns of majesty on his wheels; and a royal diadem upon his skull.

(8) And his body is full of eyes. And wings are covering the whole of his high stature (lit. the height of his stature is all wings).

(9) On his right hand a flame is burning, and on his left a fire is glowing; and coals are burning from it. And firebrands go forth from his body. And lightnings are cast forth from his face. With him there is alway thunder upon (in) thunder, by his side there is ever earthquake upon (in) earthquake.

(10) And the two princes of the Merkaba are together with him.

(11) Why is he called KERUBIEL H', the Prince. Because he is appointed over the chariot of the Kerubim. And the mighty Kerubim are given in his charge. And he adorns the crowns on their heads and polishes the diadem upon their skull.

(12) He magnifies the glory of their appearance. And he glorifies the beauty of their majesty. And he increases the greatness of their honour. He causes the song of their praise to be sung. He intensifies their beautiful strength. He causes the brilliance of their glory to shine forth. He beautifies their goodly mercy and lovingkindness. He frames the fairness of their radiance. He makes their merciful beauty even more beautiful. He glorifies their upright majesty. He extols the order of their praise, to stablish the dwellingplace of him "who dwelleth on the Kerubim".

(13) And the Kerubim are standing by the Holy Chayyoth, and their wings are raised up to their heads (lit. are as the height of their heads) and Shekina is (resting) upon them and the brillianceof the Glory is upon their faces and song and praise in their mouth and their hands are under their wings and their feet are covered by their wings and horns of glory are upon their heads and the splendour of Shekina on their face and Shekina is (resting) upon them and sapphire stones are round about them and columns of fire on their four sides and columns of firebrands beside them.

(14) There is one sapphire on one side and another sapphire on another side and under the sapphires there are coals of burning juniper.

(15) And one Kerub is standing in each direction but the wings of the Kerubim compass each other above their skulls in glory; and they spread them to sing with them a song to him that inhabiteth the clouds and to praise with them the fearful majesty of the king of kings.

(16) And KERUBIEL H', the prince who is appointed over them, he arrays them in comely, beautiful and pleasant orders and he exalts them in all manner of exaltation, dignity and glory. And he hastens them in glory and might to do the will of their Creator every moment. For above their lofty heads abides continually the glory of the high king "who dwelleth on the Kerubim".

CHAPTER XXII b
(ADDITIONAL)

(1) And there is a court before the Throne of Glory,

(2) which no seraph nor angel can enter, and it is 36,000 myriads of parasangs, as it is written (Is.vi.2): "and the Seraphim are standing above him" (the last word of the scriptural passage being 'Lamech-Vav' [numerical value: 36]).

(3) As the numerical value Lamech-Vav (36) the number of the bridges there.

(4) And there are 24 myriads of wheels of fire. And the ministering angels are 12,000 myriads. And there are 12,000 rivers of hail, and 12,000 treasuries of snow. And in the seven Halls are chariots of fire and flames, without reckoning, or end or searching.

R. Ishmael said to me: Metatron, the angel, the Prince of the Presence, said to me:

(1) How are the angels standing on high? Pie said: Like a bridge that is placed over a river so that every one can pass over it, likewise a bridge is placed from the beginning of the entry to the end.

(2) And three ministering angels surround it and utter a song before YHWH, the God of Israel. And there are standing before it lords of dread and captains of fear, thousand times thousand and ten thousand times ten thousand in number and they sing praise and hymns before YHWH, the God of Israel.

(3) Numerous bridges are there: bridges of fire and numerous bridges of hail. Also numerous rivers of hail, numerous treasuries of snow and numerous wheels offire.

(4) And how many are the ministering angels? 12,000 myriads: six (thousand myriads) above and six (thousand myriads] below. And 12,000 are the treasuries of snow, six above and six below. And 24 myriads of wheels of fire, 12 (myriads] above and 12 (myriads] below. And they surround the bridges and the rivers of fire and the rivers of hail. And there are numerous ministering angels, forming entries, for all the creatures that are standing in the midst thereof, corresponding to (over against) the paths of Raqia Shamayim.

(5) What doeth YHWH, the God of Israel, the King of Glory? The Great and Fearful God, mighty in strength, doth cover his face.

(6) In Araboth are 660,000 myriads of angels of glory standing over against the Throne of Glory and the divisions offlaming fire. And the King of Glory doth cover His face; for else the (Araboth Raqia1 would be rent asunder in its midst because of the majesty, splendour, beauty, radiance, loveliness, brilliancy, brightness and excellency of the appearance of (the Holy One,) blessed be He.

(7) There are numerous ministering angelsperforming his will, numerous kings, numerous princes in the 'Araboth of his delight, angels who are revered among the rulers in heaven, distinguished, adorned with song and bringing love to remembrance: (who) are affrighted by the splendour of the Shekina, and their eyes are dazzled by the shining beauty of their King, their faces grow black and their strength doth fail.

(8) There go forth rivers ofjoy, streams of gladness, rivers of rejoicing, streams of triumph, rivers of love, streams of friendship (another reading:) of commotion and they flow over and go forth before the Throne of Glory and wax great and go through the gates of the paths of 'Araboth Raqia at the voice of the shouting and musick of the CHAYYOTH, at the voice of the rejoicing of the timbrels of his 'OPHANNIM and at the melody of the cymbals of His Kerubim. And they wax great and go forth with commotion with the sound of the hymn: "HOLY, HOLY, HOLY, IS THE LORD OF HOSTS; THE WHOLE EARTH IS FULL OF HIS GLORY!"

CHAPTER XXII c

R. Ishmael said: Metatron, the Prince of the Presence said to me:

(1) What is the distance between one bridge and another? 12 myriads of parasangs. Their ascent is 12 myriads of parasangs, and their descent 12 myriads of parasangs.

(2) (The distance) between the rivers of dread and the rivers of fear is 22 myriads of parasangs; between the rivers of hail and the rivers of darkness 36 myriads of parasangs; between the chambers of lightnings and the clouds of compassion 42 myriads of parasangs; between the clouds of compassion and the Merkaba 84 myriads of parasangs; between the Merkaba and the Kerubim 148 myriads of parasangs; between the Kerubim and the 'Ophannim 24 myriads of parasangs; between the Ophannim and the chambers of chambers 24 myriads of parasangs; between the chambers of chambers and the Holy Chayyoth 40,000 myriads of parasangs; between one wing (of the Chayyoth) and another 12 myriads of parasangs; and the breadth of each one wing is of that same measure; and the distance between the Holy Chayyoth and the Throne of Glory is 30,000 myriads of parasangs.

(3) And from the foot of the Throne to the seat there are 40,000 myriads of parasangs. And the name of Him that sitteth on it: let the name be sanctified!

(4) And the arches of the Bow are set above the 'Araboth, and they are 1000 thousands and 10,000 times ten thousands (of parasangs) high. Their measure is after the measure of the 'Irin and Qaddishin (Watchers and Holy Ones). As it is written (Gen. ix. 13) "My bow I have set in the cloud". It is not written here "I will set" but "I have set", (i.e.) already; clouds that surround the Throne of Glory. As His clouds pass by, the angels of hail (turn into) burning coal.

(5) And a fire of the voice goes down from by the Holy Chayyoth. And because of the breath of that voice they "run" (Ezek. i. 14) to another place, fearing lest it command them to go; and they "return" lest it injure them from the other side. Therefore "they run and return" (Ezek. i. 14).

(6) And these arches of the Bow are more beautiful and radiant than the radiance of the sun during the summer solstice. And they are whiter than a flaming fire and they are great and beautiful.

(7) Above the arches of the Bow are the wheels of the 'Ophannim. Their height is 1000 thousand and 10,000 times 10,000 units of measure after the measure of the Seraphim and the Troops (Gedudim).

CHAPTER XXIII

The winds blowing under the wings of the Kerubim

R. Ishmael said: Metatron, the Angel, the Prince of the Presence, said to me:

(1) There are numerous winds blowing under the wings of the Kerubim.

There blows "the Brooding Wind", as it is written (Gen. i. 2): " and the wind of God was brooding upon the face of the waters ".

(2) There blows "the Strong Wind", as it is said (Ex. xiv. 21): "and the Lord caused the sea to go back by a strong east wind all that night".

(3) There blows "the East Wind"as it is written (Ex. x. 13): "the east wind brought the locusts".

(4) There blows "the Wind of Quails" as it is written (Num. xi. 31): "And there went forth a wind from the Lord and brought quails".

(5) There blows "the Wind of Jealousy" as it is written (Num.v.14): "And the wind of jealousy came upon him".

(6) There blows the "Wind of Earthquake" as it is written (i Kings .xix. 1 1): "and after that the wind of the earthquake; but the Lord was not in the earthquake".

(7) There blows the "Wind of H' " as it is written (Ex. xxxvii. i): "and he carried me out by the wind of H' and set me down".

(8) There blows the "Evil Wind " as it is written (i Sam. xvi. 23): "and the evil wind departed from him".

(9) There blow the "Wind of Wisdom" 5and the "Wind of Understanding" and the "Wind of Knowledge" and the "Wind of the Fear of H'" as it is written (Is. xi. 2): "And the wind of H'shall rest upon him; the wind of wisdom and understanding, the wind of counsel and might, the wind of knowledge and of the fear.

(10) There blows the "Wind of Rain", as it is written (Prov. xxv. 23): "the north wind bringeth forth rain".

(11) There blows the "Wind of Lightnings ", as it is written (Jer.x.13, li. 16): "he maketh lightnings for the rain and bringeth forth the wind out of his treasuries ".

(12) There blows the "Wind, Breaking the Rocks", as it is written (i Kings xix. n): "the Lord passed by and a great and strong wind (rent the mountains and brake in pieces the rocks before the Lord)".

(13) There blows the "Wind of Assuagement of the Sea", as it is written (Gen. viii. i): "and God made a wind to pass over the earth, and the waters assuaged".

(14) There blows the "Wind of Wrath", as it is written (Job i. 19): "and behold there came a great wind from the wilderness and smote the four corners of the house and it fell".

(15) There blows the " Storm-Wind ", as it is written (Ps. cxlviii. 8): "Storm-wind, fulfilling his word".

(16) And Satan is standing among these winds, for "storm-wind " is nothing else but "Satan", and all these winds do not blow but under the wings of the Kerubim, as it is written (Ps. xviii. n): "and he rode upon a cherub and did fly, yea, and he flew swiftly upon the wings of the wind".

(17) And whither go all these winds? The Scripture teaches us, that they go out from under the wings of the Kerubim and descend on the globe of the sun, as it is written (Eccl. i. 6): " The wind goeth toward the south and turneth about unto the north ; it turneth about continually in its course and the wind 14 returneth again to its circuits ". And from the globe of the sun they return and descend upon the rivers and the seas, upon] the mountains and upon the hills, as it is written (Am.iv.13): "For lo, he that formeth the mountains and createth the wind".

(18) And from the mountains and the hills they return and descend to the seas and the rivers ; and from the seas and the rivers they return and descend upon (the) cities and provinces ; and from the cities and provinces they return and descend into the Garden, and from the Garden they return and descend to Eden, as it is written (Gen.iii. 8): "walking in the Garden in the wind of day". And in the midst of the Garden they join together and blow from one side to the other and are perfumed with the spices of the Garden even from \ts remotest parts, until they separate from each other, and, filled with the scent of the pure spices, they bring the odour from the remotest parts of Eden and the spices of the Garden to the righteous and godly who in the time to come shall inherit the Garden of Eden and the Tree of Life, as it is written (Cant. iv. 16): "Awake, O north wind; and come thou south; blow upon my garden, that the spices thereof may flow out. Let my beloved come into his garden and eat his precious fruits".

CHAPTER XXIV

The different chariots of the Holy One, blessed be He

R. Ishmael said: Metatron, the Angel, the Prince of the Presence, the glory of all heaven, said to me:

(1) Numerous chariots has the Holy One, blessed be He:

He has the "Chariots of (the) Kerubim", as it is written (Ps.xviii.11, 2 Sam.xxii.11): "And he rode upon a cherub and did fly".

(2) He has the "Chariots of Wind", as it is written (ib.): "and he flew swiftly upon the wings of the wind ".

(3) He has the "Chariots of (the) Swift Cloud", as it is written (Is. xix. i): "Behold, the Lord rideth upon a swift cloud".

(4) He has "the Chariots of Clouds", as it is written (Ex. xix. 9): "Lo, I come unto thee in a cloud".

(5) He has the "Chariots of the Altar", as it is written (Am. ix. i):"I saw the Lord standing upon the Altar".

(6) He has the "Chariots of Ribbotaim", as it is written (Ps.lxviii. 18): "The chariots of God are Ribbotaim ; thousands of angels ".

(7) He has the "Chariots of the Tent", as it is written (Deut.xxxi. 15): "And the Lord appeared in the Tent in a pillar of cloud ".

(8) He has the "Chariots of the Tabernacle", as it is written (Lev. i. **1**): "And the Lord spake unto him out of the tabernacle".

(9) He has the "Chariots of the Mercy-Seat", as it is written (Num. vii. 89): "then he heard the Voice speaking unto him from upon the mercy-seat".

(10) He has the "Chariots of Sapphire Stone", as it is written (Ex. xxiv. 10): "and there was under his feet as it were a paved work of sapphire stone".

(11) He has the "Chariots of Eagles ", as it is written (Ex. xix. 4):"I bare you on eagles' wings". Eagles literally are not meant here but "they that fly swiftly as eagles".

(12) He has the "chariots of Shout", as it is written (Ps. xlvii. 6):"God is gone up with a shout".

(13) He has the "Chariots of 'Araboth", as it is written (Ps.Ixviii. 5): "Extol Him that rideth upon the 'Araboth".

(14) He has the "Chariots of Thick Clouds", as it is written (Ps. civ. 3): "who maketh the thick clouds His chariot".

(15) He has the "Chariots of the Chayyoth", as it is written (Ezek. i. 14): "and the Chayyoth ran and returned". They run by permission and return by permission, for Shekina is above their heads.

(16) He has the "Chariots of Wheels (Galgallim)", as it is written (Ezek. x. 2): "And he said: Go in between the whirling wheels".

(17) lie has the "Chariots of a Swift Kerub", as it is written (Ps.xviii.10 & Is.xix.1): "riding on a swift cherub".

And at the time when He rides on a swift kerub, as he sets one of His feet upon him, before he sets the other foot upon his back, he looks through eighteen thousand worlds at one glance. And he discerns and sees into them all and knows what is in all of them and then he sets down the other foot upon him, according as it is written (Ezek. xlviii. 35): "Round about eighteen thousand".

Whence do we know that He looks through every one of them every day? It is written (Ps. xiv. 2): "He looked down from heaven upon the children of men to see if there were any that did understand, that did seek after God".

(18) He has the "Chariots of the 'Ophannim", as it is written (Ezek. x. 12): "and the 'Ophannim were full of eyes round about". 12

(19) He has the "Chariots of His Holy Throne", as it is written (Ps. xlvii. 8):" God sitteth upon his holy throne ".

(20) He has the "chariots of the Throne of Yah", as it is written (Ex. xvii. 16): "Because a hand is lifted up upon the Throne of Jah".

(21) He has the "Chariots of the Throne of Judgement", as it is written (Is. v. 16): "but the Lord of hosts shall be exalted in judgment".

(22) He has the "Chariots of the Throne of Glory ", as it is written (Jer. xvii. 12): "The Throne of Glory, set on high from the beginning, is the place of our sanctuary".

(23) He has the "Chariots of the High and Exalted Throne", as it is written (Is. vi. i): "I saw the Lord sitting upon the high and exalted throne".

CHAPTER XXV

'Ophphanniel, the prince of the 'Ophannim. Description of the 'Ophannim

R. Ishmael said: Metatron, the Angel, the Prince of the Presence, said to me:

(1) Above these there is one great prince, revered, high, lordly, fearful, ancient and strong. 'OPHPHANNIEL H is his name.

(2) He has sixteen faces, four faces on each side,(also) hundred wings on each side. And he has 8466 eyes, corresponding to the days of the year. [2190 –and some say 2116- on each side.] [2191 /2196 and sixteen on each side.]

(3) And those two eyes of his face, in each one of them lightnings are flashing, and from each one of them firebrands are burning ; and no creature is able to behold them: for anyone who looks at them is burnt instantly.

(4) His height is (as) the distance of 2500 years' journey. No eye can behold and no mouth can tell the mighty power of his strength save the King of kings, the Holy One, blessed be He, alone.

(5) Why is he called 'OPHPHAN-NIEL ? Because he is appointed over the 'Ophannim and the 'Ophannimare given in his charge. He stands every day and attends and beautifies them. And he exalts and orders their apartment and polishes their standingplace and makes bright their dwellings, makes their corners even and cleanses their seats. And he waits upon them early and late, by day and by night, to increase their beauty, to make great their dignity and to make them "diligent in praise of their Creator.

(6) And all the 'Ophannim are full of eyes, and they are all full of brightness; seventy two sapphire stones are fixed on their garments on their right side and seventy two sapphire stones are fixed on their garments on their left side.

(7) And four carbuncle stones are fixed on the crown of every single one, the splendour of which proceeds in the four directions of 'Araboth even as the splendour of the globe of the sun proceeds in all the directions of the universe. And why is it called Carbuncle (Bareqet)? Because its splendour is like the appearance of a lightning (Baraq). And tents of splendour, tents of brilliance, tents of brightness as of sapphire and carbuncle inclose them because of the shining appearance of their eyes.

CHAPTER XXVI

SERAPHIEL, the Prince of the Seraphim. Description of the Seraphim

R. Ishmael said: Metatron, the Angel, the Prince of the Presence, said to me:

(1) Above these there is one prince, wonderful, noble, great, honourable, mighty, terrible, a chief and leader 1 and a swift scribe, glorified, honoured and beloved.

(2) He is altogether filled with splendour, full of praise and shining; and he is wholly full of brilliance, of light and of beauty; and the whole of him is filled with goodliness and greatness.

(3) His countenance is altogether like (that of) angels, but his body is like an eagle's body.

(4) His splendour is like unto lightnings, his appearance like fire brands, his beauty like unto sparks, his honour like fiery coals, his majesty like chashmals, his radiance like the light of the planet Venus.

The image of him is like unto the Greater Light. His height is as the seven heavens. The light from his eyebrows is like the sevenfold light.

(5) The sapphire stone upon his head is as great as the whole universe and like unto the splendour of the very heavens in radiance.

(6) His body is full of eyes like the stars of the sky, innumerable and unsearchable. Every eye is like the planet Venus. Yet, there are some of them like the Lesser Light and some of them like unto the Greater Light. From his ankles to his knees (they are) like unto stars of lightning, from his knees to his thighs like unto the planet Venus, from his thighs to his loins like unto the moon, from his loins to his neck like the sun, from his neck to his skull like unto the Light Imperishable. (Cf. Zeph. iii. 5.)

(7) The crown on his head is like unto the splendour of the Throne of Glory. The measure of the crown is the distance of 502 years' journey. There is no kind of splendour, no kind of brilliance, no kind of radiance, no kind of light in the universe but is fixed on that crown.

(8) The name of that prince is SERAPHIEL H". And the crown on his head, its name is "the Prince of Peace". And why is he called by the name of SERAPHIEL '? Because he is appointed over the Seraphim. And the flaming Seraphim are given in his charge. And he presides over them by day and by night and teaches them song, praise, proclamation of beauty, might and majesty; that they may proclaim the beauty of their King in all manner of Praise and Sanctification (Qedushsha).

(9) How many are the Seraphim? Four, corresponding to the four winds of the world. And how many wings have they each one of them? Six, corresponding to the six days of Creation. And how many faces have they? Each one of them four faces.

(10) The measure of the Seraphim and the height of each one of them correspond to the height of the seven heavens. The size of each wing is like the measure of all Raqia' . The size of each face is like that of the face of the East.

(11) And each one of them gives forth light like unto the splendour of the Throne of Glory: so that not even the Holy Chayyoth, the honoured 'Ophannim, nor the majestic KeruUm are able to behold it. For everyone who beholds it, his eyes are darkened because of its great splendour.

(12) Why are they called Seraphim? Because they burn (saraph) the writing tables of Satan: Every day Satan is sitting, together with SAMMAEL, the Prince of Rome, and with DUBBIEL, the Prince of Persia, and they write the iniquities of Israel on writing tables which they hand over to the Seraphim, in order that they may present them before the Holy One, blessed be He, so that He may destroy Israel from the world. But the Seraphim know from the secrets of the Holy One, blessed be He, that he desires not, that this people Israel should perish. What do the Seraphim? Every day do they receive (accept) them from the hand of Satan and burn them in the burning fire over against the high and exalted Throne in order that they may not come before the Holy One, blessed be He, at the time when he is sitting upon the Throne of Judgement, judging the whole world in truth.

CHAPTER XXVII

RADWERIEL, the keeper of the Book of Records

R. Ishmael said: Metatron, the Angel of H', the Prince of the Presence, said to me:

(1) Above the Seraphim there is one prince, exalted above all the princes, wondrous more than all the servants. His name is RADWERIEL H' who is appointed over the treasuries of the books.

(2) He fetches forth the Case of Writings (with) the Book of Records in it, and brings it before the Holy One, blessed be He. And he breaks the seals of the case, opens it, takes out the books and delivers them before the Holy One, blessed be He. And the Holy One, blessed be He, receives them of his hand and gives them in his sight to the Scribes, that they may read them in the Great Beth Din (The court of justice) in the height of 'Araboth Raqia', before the heavenly household.

(3) And why is he called RADWERIEL? Because out of every word that goes forth from his mouth an angel is created: and he stands in the songs (in the singing company) of the ministering angels and utters a song before the Holy One, blessed be He when the time draws nigh for the recitation of the (Thrice) Holy.

CHAPTER XXVIII

The 'Irin and Qaddishin

R. Ishmael said: Metatron, the Angel, the Prince of the Presence, said to me:

(1) Above all these there are four great princes, Irin and Qaddishin by name: high, honoured, revered, beloved, wonderful and glorious ones, greater than all the children of heaven. There is none like unto them among all the celestial princes and none their equal among all the Servants. For each one of them is equal to all the rest together.

(2) And their dwelling is over against the Throne of Glory, and their standing place over against the Holy One, blessed be He, so that the brilliance of their dwelling is a reflection of the brilliance of the Throne of Glory. And the splendour of their countenance is a reflection of the splendour of Shekina.

(3) And they are glorified by the glory of 4the Divine Majesty (Gebura) and praised by (through) the praise of Shekina.

(4) And not only that, but the Holy One, blessed be He, does nothing in his world without first consulting them, but after that he doeth it. As it is written (Dan. iv. 17): "The sentence is by the decree of the 'Irin and the demand by the word of the Qaddishin."

(5) The Ilrin are two and the Qaddishin are two. And how are they standing before the Holy One, blessed be He? It is to be understood, that one 'Ir is standing on one side and the other 'Ir on the other side, and one Qaddish is standing on one side and the other on the other side.

(6) And ever do they exalt the humble, and they abase to the ground those that are proud, and they exalt to the height those that are humble.

(7) And every day, as the Holy One, blessed be He, is sitting upon the Throne of Judgement and judges the whole world, and the Books of the Living and the Books of the Dead are opened before Him, then all the children of heaven are standing before him in fear, dread, awe and trembling. At that time, (when) the Holy One, blessed be He, is sitting upon the Throne of Judgement to execute judgement, his garment is white as snow, the hair on his head as pure wool and the whole of his cloak is like the shining light. And he is covered with righteousness all over as with a coat of mail.

(8) And those 'Irm and Qaddishin are standing before him like court officers before the judge. And they raise and argue every case and close the case that comes before the Holy One, blessed be He, in judgement, according as it is written (Dan. iv. 17): "The sentence is by the decree of the 'Irm and the demand by the word of the Qaddishin"

(9) Some of them argue and others pass the sentence in the Great Beth Din in 'Araboth. Some of them make the requests from before uthe Divine Majesty and some close the cases before the Most

High. Others finish by going down and (confirming) executing the sentences on earth below. According as it is written (Dan. iv. 13 , 14): " Behold an 'Ir and a Qaddishcame down from heaven and cried aloud and said thus, Hew down the tree, and cut off his branches, shake off his leaves, and scatter his fruit: let the beasts get away from under it, and the fowls from his branches ".

(10) Why are they called 'Irin and Qaddishint By reason that they sanctify the body and the spirit with lashes of fire on the third day of the judgement, as it is written (Hos. vi. 2):

"After two days will he revive us: on the third he will raise us up, and we shall live before him."

CHAPTER XXIX

Description of a class of angels

R. Ishmael said: Metatron, the Angel, the Prince of the Presence,said to me:

(1) Each one of them has seventy names corresponding to the seventy tongues of the world. And all of them are (based) upon the name of the Holy One, blessed be He. And every several name is written with a flaming style upon the Fearful Crown (Keiher Nora) which is on the head of the high and exalted King.

(2) And from each one of them there go forth sparks and lightnings. And each one of them is beset with horns of splendour round about. From each one lights are shining forth, and each one is surrounded by tents of brilliance so that not even the Seraphim and the Chayyoth who are greater than all the children of heaven are able to behold them.

CHAPTER XXX

The 72 princes of Kingdoms and the Prince of the World officiating at the Great Sanhedrin in heaven

R. Ishmael said: Metatron, the Angel, the Prince of the Presence, said to me:

(1) Whenever the Great Beth Din is seated in the 'Araboth Raqia' on high there is no opening of the mouth for anyone in the world save those great princes who are called H' by the name of the Holy One, blessed be He.

(2) How many are those princes? Seventytwo princes of the kingdoms of the world besides the Prince of the World who speaks (pleads) in favour of the world before the Holy One, blessed be He, every day, at the hour when the book is opened in which are recorded all the doings of the world, according as it is written (Dan.vii.10): "The judgement was set and the books were opened."

CHAPTER XXXI

(The attributes of) Justice, Mercy and Truth by the Throne of Judgement

R. Ishmael said: Metatron, the Angel, the Prince of the Presence,said to me:

(1) At the time when the Holy One, blessed be He, is sitting on the Throne, of Judgement, (then) Justice is standing on His right and Mercy on His left and Truth before His face.

(2) And when man enters before Him to judgement,(then) there comes forth from the splendour of the Mercy towards him as (it were) a staff and stands in front of him. Forthwith man falls upon his face, (and) all the angels of destruction fear and tremble before him, according as it is written (Is.xvi. 5): "And with mercy shall the throne be established, and he shall sit upon it in truth."

CHAPTER XXXII

The execution of judgement on the wicked. God's sword

R. Ishmael said: Metatron, the Angel, the Prince of the Presence, said to me:

(1) When the Holy One, blessed be He, opens the Book half of which is fire and half flame, (then) they go out from before Him in every moment to execute the judgement on the wicked by His sword (that is) drawn forth out of its sheath and the splendour of which shines like a lightning and pervades the world from one end to the other, as it is written (Is. lxvi. 16): "For by fire will the Lord plead (and by his sword with all flesh)."

(2) And all the inhabitants of the world (lit. those who come into the world) fear and tremble before Him, when they behold His sharpened sword like unto a lightning from one end of the world to the other, and sparks and flashes of the size of the stars of Raqia' going out from it; according as it is written (Deut. xxxii. 41):" If I whet the lightning of my sword".

CHAPTER XXXIII

The angels of Mercy, of Peace and of Destruction by the Throne of Judgement.
The scribes, (vss. i, 2) The angels by the Throne of Glory and the fiery rivers under it. (vss. 3-5)

R. Ishmael said: Metatron, the Angel, the Prince of the Presence, said to me:

(1) At the time that the Holy One, blessed be He, is sitting on the Throne of Judgement, (then) the angels of Mercy are standing on His right, the angels of Peace are standing on His left and the angels of Destruction are standing in front of Him.

(2) And one scribe is standing beneath Him, and another scribe above Him. (3) And the glorious Seraphim surround the Throne on its four sides with walls of lightnings, and the 'Ophannim. surround them with fire-brands round about the Throne of Glory. And clouds of fire and clouds of flames compass them to the right and to the left; and the Holy Chayyoth carry the Throne of Glory from below: each one with three fingers. The measure of the fingers of each one is 800,000 and 700 times hundred, (and) 66,000 parasangs.

(3) And underneath the feet of the Chayyoth seven fiery rivers are running and flowing. And the breadth of each river is 365 thousand parasangs and its depth is 248 thousand myriads of parasangs. Its length is unsearchable and immeasureable.

(4) And each river turns round in a bow in the four directions of 'Araboth Raqict , and (from there) it falls down to Ma'on and is stayed, and from Ma1 on to Zebul, from Zebul to Shechaqim, from Shechaqim to Raqia' , from Raqia' to Shamayim and from Shamayim upon the heads of the wicked who are in Gehenna, as it is written (Jer. xxiii. 19): "Behold a whirlwind of the Lord, even his fury, is gone, yea, a whirling tempest; it shall burst upon the head of the wicked".

CHAPTER XXXIV

The different concentric circles round the Chayyoth, consisting of fire, water, hailstones etc. and of the angels uttering the Qedushsha responsorium

R. Ishmael said: Metatron; the Angel, the Prince of the Presence, said to me:

(1) The hoofs of the Chayyoth are surrounded by seven clouds of burning coals. The clouds of burning coals are surrounded on the outside by seven walls of flame(s). The seven walls of flame(s) are surrounded on the outside by seven walls of hailstones (stones of 'Et-gabish, Ezek. xiii. 11,13, xxviii. 22). The hailstones are surrounded on the outside by xstones of hail (stone of Barad). The stones of hail are surrounded on the outside by stones of "the wings of the tempest ".

The stones of "the wings of the tempest" are surrounded on the outside by flames of fire. The flames of fire are surrounded by the chambers of the whirlwind. The chambers of the whirlwind are surrounded on the outside by the fire and the water.

(2) Round about the fire and the water are those who utter the "Holy". Round about those who utter the "Holy" are those who utter the "Blessed'". Round about those who utter the "Blessed" are the bright clouds. The bright clouds are surrounded on the outside by coals of burning jumper ; and on the outside surrounding the coals of burning juniper there are thousand camps of fire and ten thousand hosts of flame(s). And between every several camp and every several host there is a cloud, so that they may not be burnt by the fire.

CHAPTER XXXV

The camps of angels in 'Araboth Raqia: angels, performing the Qedushsha

R. Ishmael said: Metatron, the Angel, the Prince of the Presence, said to me:

(1) 506 thousand myriads of camps has the Holy One, blessed be He, in the height of 'Araboth Raqia. And each camp is

(composed of) 496 thousand angels.

(2) And every single angel, the height of his stature is as the great sea; and the appearance of their countenance as the appearance of the lightning, and their eyes as lamps of fire, and their arms and their feet like in colour to polished brass and the roaring voice of their words like the voice of a multitude.

(3) And they are all standing before the Throne of Glory in four rows. And the princes of the army are standing at the head of each row.

(4) And some of them utter the "Holy" and others utter the "Blessed", some of them run as messengers, others are standing in attendance, according as it is written (Dan. vii. 10): "Thousand thousands ministered unto him, and ten thousand times ten thousand stood before him: the judgment was set and the books were opened ".

(5) And in the hour, when the time draws nigh for to say the "Holy", (then) first there goes forth a whirlwind from before the Holy One, blessed be He, and bursts upon the camp of Shekina and there arises a great commotion among them, as it is written (Jer.xxx. 23): "Behold, the whirlwind of the Lord goeth forth with fury, a continuing commotion".

(6) At that moment 4thousand thousands of them are changed into sparks, thousand thousands of them into firebrands, thousand thousands into flashes, thousand thousands into flames, thousand thousands into males, thousand thousands into females, thousand thousands into winds, thousand thousands into burning fires, thousand thousands into flames, thousand thousands into sparks, thousand thousands into chashmals of light; until they take upon themselves the yoke of the kingdom of heaven, the high and lifted up, of the Creator of them all with fear, dread, awe and trembling, with commotion, anguish, terror and trepidation. Then they are changed again into their former shape to have the fear of their King before them alway, as they have set their hearts on saying the Song continually, as it is written (Is. vi. 3): "And one cried unto another and said (Holy, Holy, Holy, etc.)".

CHAPTER XXXVI

The angels bathe in the fiery river before reciting the 'Song'

R. Ishmael said: Metatron, the Angel, the Prince of the Presence, said to me:

(1) At the time when the ministering angels desire to say (the) Song, (then) Nehar di-Nur (the fiery stream) rises with many thousand thousands and myriads of myriads" (of angels) of power and strength of fire and it runs and passes under the Throne of Glory, between the camps of the ministering angels and the troops of 'Araboth.

(1) And all the ministering angels first go down into Nehar di-Nur, and they dip themselves in the fire and dip their tongue and their mouth seven times ; and after that they go up and put on the garment of 'Machaqe Samal' and cover themselves with cloaks of chashmal and stand in four rows over against the Throne of Glory, in all the heavens.

CHAPTER XXXVII

The four camps of Shekina and their surroundings

R. Ishmael said: Metatron, the Angel, the Prince of the Presence, said to me:

(1) In the seven Halls there are standing four chariots of Shekina, and before each one are standing the four camps of Shekina. Between each camp a river of fire is continually flowing.

(2) Between each river there are bright clouds [surrounding them], and between each cloud there are put up pillars of brimstone. Between one pillar and another there are standing flaming wheels, surrounding them. And between one wheel and another there are flames of fire round about. Between one flame and another there are treasuries of lightnings; behind the treasuries of lightnings are the wings of the stormwind. Behind the wings of the stormwind are the chambers of the tempest; behind the chambers of the tempest there are winds, voices, thunders, sparks [upon] sparks and earthquakes [upon] earthquakes.

CHAPTER XXXVIII

The fear that befalls all the heavens at the sound of the 'Holy? esp. the heavenly bodies. These appeased by the Prince of the World

R. Ishmael said: Metatron, the Angel, the Prince of the Presence, said to me:

(1) At the time, when the ministering angels utter (the Thrice) Holy, then all the pillars of the heavens and their sockets do tremble, and the gates of the Halls of Araboth Raqia' are shaken and the foundations of Shechaqim and the Universe (Tebel) are moved, and the orders of Ma'on and the chambers of Makon quiver, and all the orders of Raqia and the constellations and the planets are dismayed, and the globes of the sun and the moon haste away and flee out of their courses and run 12,000 parasangs and seek to throw themselves down from heaven,

(2) by reason of the roaring voice of their chant, and the noise of their praise and the sparks and lightnings that go forth from their faces; as it is written (Ps. lxxvii. 18): "The voice of thy thunder was in the heaven (the lightnings lightened the world, the earth trembled and shook) ".

(3) Until the prince of the world calls them, saying: "Be ye quiet in your place ! Fear not because of the ministering angels who sing the Song before the Holy One, blessed be He". As it is written (Job.xxxviii. 7): "When the morning stars sang together and all the children of heaven shouted for joy".

CHAPTER XXXIX

The explicit names fly offfrom the Throne and all the various angelic hosts prostrate themselves before it at the time of the Qedushsha

R. Ishmael said: Metatron, the Angel, the Prince of the Presence, said to me:

(1) When the ministering angels utter the "Holy" then all the explicit names that are graven with a flaming style on the Throne of Glory fly off like eagles, with sixteen wings. And they surround and compass the Holy One, blessed be He, on the four sides of the place of His Shekina1.

(2) And the angels of the host, and the flaming Servants, and the mighty 'Ophannim, and the Kerubim of the Shekina, and the Holy Chayyoth, and the Seraphim, and the 'Er'ellim, and the Taphsarim and the troops of consuming fire, and the fiery armies, and the flaming hosts, and the holy princes, adorned with crowns, clad in kingly majesty, wrapped in glory, girt with loftiness, 4 fall upon their faces three times, saying: "Blessed be the name of His glorious kingdom for ever and ever".

CHAPTER XL

The ministering angels rewarded with crowns, when uttering the "Holy" in its right order, and punished by consuming fire if not. New ones created in the stead of the consumed angels

R. Ishmael said: Metatron, the Angel, the Prince of the Presence, said to me:

(1) When the ministering angels say "Holy" before the Holy One, blessed be He, in the proper way, then the servants of His Throne, the attendants of His Glory, go forth with great mirth from under the Throne of Glory.

(2) And they all carry in their hands, each one of them thousand thousand and ten thousand times ten thousand crowns of stars, similar in appearance to the planet Venus, and put them on the ministering angels and the great princes who utter the "Holy". Three crowns they put on each one of them: one crown because they say "Holy", another crown, because they say "Holy, Holy", and a third crown because they say "Holy, Holy, Holy, is the Lord of Hosts" .

(3) And in the moment that they do not utter the "Holy" in the right order, a consuming fire goes forth from the little finger of the Holy One, blessed be He, and falls down in the midst of their ranks and is divided into 496 thousand parts corresponding to the four camps of the ministering angels, and consumes them in one moment, as it is written (Ps. xcvii. 3): "A fire goeth before him and burneth up his adversaries round about".

(4) After that the Holy One, blessed be He, opens His mouth and speaks one word and creates others in their stead, new ones like them. And each one stands before His Throne of Glory, uttering the "Holy", as it is written (Lam. iii. 23): "They are new every morning; great is thy faithfulness".

CHAPTER XLI

Metatron shows R. Ishmael the letters engraved on the Throne of Glory by which letters everything in heaven and earth has been created

R. Ishmael said: Metatron, the Angel, the Prince of the Presence, said to me:

(1) Come and behold the letters by which the heaven and the earth were created, the letters by which were created the mountains and hills, the letters by which were created the seas and rivers, the letters by which were created the trees and herbs, the letters by which were created the planets and the constellations, the letters by which were created the globe of the moon and the globe of the sun, Orion, the Pleiades and all the different luminaries of Raqia' .

(2) the letters by which were created the Throne of Glory and the Wheels of the Merkaba, the letters by which were created the necessities of the worlds,

(3) the letters by which were created wisdom, understanding, knowledge, prudence, meekness and righteousness by which the whole world is sustained.

(4) And I walked by his side and he took me by his hand and raised me upon his wings and showed me those letters, all of them, that are graven with a flaming style on the Throne of Glory: and sparks go forth from them and cover all the chambers of 'Araboth.

CHAPTER XLII

Instances of polar opposites kept in balance by several Divine Names and other similar wonders

R. Ishmael said: Metatron, the Angel, the Prince of the Presence, said to me:

(1) Come and I will show thee, where the waters are suspended in the highest, where fire is burning in the midst of hail, where lightnings lighten out of the midst of snowy mountains, where thunders are roaring in the celestial heights, where a flame is burning in the midst of the burning fire and where voices make themselves heard in the midst of thunder and earthquake.

(2) Then I went by his side and he took me by his hand and lifted me up on his wings and showed me all those things. I beheld the waters suspended on high in 'Araboth Raqia' by (force of) the name YAH 'EHYE 'ASHER 'EHYE (Jah, I am that I am), And their fruits going down from heaven and watering the face of the world, as it is written (Ps.civ.13): "(He watereth the mountains from his chambers:) the earth is satisfied with the fruit of thy work".

(3) And I saw fire and snow and hailstone that were mingled together within each other and yet were undamaged, by (force of) the name 'ESH 'OKELA (consuming fire), as it is written (Deut. iv. 24): "For the Lord, thy God, is a consuming fire".

(4) And I saw lightnings that were lightening out of mountains of snow and yet were not damaged (quenched), by (force of) the name YAH SUR 'OLAMIM (Jah, the everlasting rock), as it is written (Is. xxvi. 4): "For in Jah, YHWH, the everlasting rock".

(5) And I saw thunders and voices that were roaring in the midst of fiety flames and were not damaged (silenced), by (force of) the name 'EL-SHADDAI RABBA (the Great God Almighty) as it is written (Gen. xvii. i): "I am God Almighty".

(6) And I beheld a flame (and) a glow (glowing flames) that were flaming and glowing in the midst of burning fire, and yet were not damaged (devoured), by (force of) the name YAD 'AL KES YAH (the hand upon the Throne of the Lord) as it is written (Ex. xvii. 16): " And he said: for the hand is upon the Throne of the Lord ".

(7) And I beheld rivers of fire in the midst of rivers of water and they were not damaged (quenched) by (force of) the name 'OSE SHALOM (Maker of Peace) as it is written (Job xxv. 2): "He maketh peace in his high places". For he makes peace between the fire and the water, between the hail and the fire, between the wind and the cloud, between the earthquake and the sparks.

CHAPTER XLIII

Metatron shows R. Ishmael the abode of the unborn spirits and of the spirits of the righteous dead

R. Ishmael said: Metatron said to me:

(1) Come and I will show thee 1where are1 the spirits of the righteous that have been created and have returned, and the spirits of the righteous that have not yet been created.

(2) And he lifted me up to his side, took me by his hand and lifted me up near the Throne of Glory by the place of the Shekina ; and he revealed the Throne of Glory to me, and he showed me the spirits that have been created and had returned: and they were flying above the Throne of Glory before the Holy One, blessed be He.

(3) After that I went to interpret the following verse of Scripture and I found in what is written (Isa.lvii. 16): "for the spirit clothed itself before me, and the souls I have made" that ("for the spirit was clothed before me") means the spirits that have been created in the chamber of creation of the righteous and that have returned before the Holy One, blessed be He; (and the words:) "and the souls I have made" refer to the spirits 4 of the righteous that have not yet been created in the chamber (GUPH).

CHAPTER XLIV

Metatron shows R. Ishmael the abode of the wicked and the intermediate in Sheol. (vss. 1-6) The Patriarchs pray for the deliverance of Israel (vss. 7-10)

R. Ishmael said: Metatron, x the Angel, the Prince of the Presence, said to me:

(1) Come and I will show thee the spirits of the wicked and the spirits of the intermediate where they are standing, and the spirits of the intermediate, whither they go down, 3and the spirits of the wicked, where they go down.

(2) And he said to me: The spirits of the wicked go down to She'ol by the hands of two angels of destruction: ZA'APHIEL and SIMKIEL are their names.

(3) SIMKIEL is appointed over the intermediate to support them and purify them because of the great mercy of the Prince of the Place (Maqom). ZA'APHIEL is appointed over the spirits of the wicked in order to cast them down from the presence of the Holy One, blessed be He, and from the splendour of the Shekina to She'ol, to be punished in the fire of Gehenna with staves of burning coal.

(4) And I went by his side, and he took me by his hand and showed me all of them with his fingers.

(5) And I beheld the appearance of their faces (and, lo, it was) as the appearance of children of men, and their bodies like eagles.

And not only that but (furthermore) the colour of the countenance of the intermediate was like pale grey on account of their deeds, for there are stains upon them until they have become cleaned from their iniquity in the fire.

(6) And the colour of the wicked was like the bottom of a pot on account of the wickedness of their doings.

(7) And I saw the spirits of the Patriarchs Abraham Isaac and Jacob and the rest of the righteous whom they have brought up out of their graves and who have ascended to the Heaven (Raqirf). And they were praying before the Holy One, blessed be He, saying intheir prayer: "Lord of the Universe! How long wilt thou sit upon (thy) Throne like a mourner in the days of his mourning with thy right hand behind thee 7and not7 deliver thy children and reveal thy Kingdom in the world? And for how long wilt thou have no pity upon thy children who are made slaves among the nations of the world? Nor upon thy right hand that is behind thee wherewith thou didst stretch out the heavens and the earth and the heavens of heavens? When wilt thou have compassion?"

(8) Then the Holy One, blessed be He, answered every one of them, saying: "Since these wicked do sin so and so, and transgress with such and such transgressions against me, how could I deliver my great Right Hand in the downfall by their hands (caused by them).

(9) In that moment Metatron called me and spake to me: "My servant! Take the books, and read their evil doings!" Forthwith I took the books and read their doings and there were to be found 36 transgressions (written down) with regard to each wicked one and besides, that they have transgressed all the letters in the Tora, as it is written (Dan. ix. u): "Yea, all Israel have transgressed thy Law". It is not written 'al torateka but 'et (JIN) torateka, for they have transgressed from 'Aleph to Taw, 4O statutes have they transgressed for each letter.

(10) Forthwith Abraham, Isaac and Jacob wept. Then said to them the Holy One, blessed be He: "Abraham, my beloved, Isaac, my Elect one, Jacob, my firstborn!

How can I now deliver them from among the nations of the world?" And forthwith MIKAEL, the Prince of Israel, cried and wept with a loud voice and said (Ps. x. i):

"Why standest thou afar off, O Lord?".

CHAPTER XLV

Metatron shows R. Ishmael past andfuture events recorded on the Curtain of the Throne

R. Ishmael said: Metatron said to me:

(1) Come, and I will show thee the Curtain of MAQOM (the Divine Majesty) which is spread before the Holy One, blessed be He, (and) whereon are graven all the generations of the world and all their doings, both what they have done and what they will do until the end of all generations.

(2) And I went, and he showed it to me pointing it out with his fingers Mike a father who teaches his children the letters of Tora. And I saw each generation, the rulers of each generation, and the heads of each generation, the shepherds of each generation, the oppressors (drivers) of each generation, the keepers of each generation, the scourgers of each generation, the overseers of each generation, the judges of each generation, the court officers of each generation , the teachers of each generation, the supporters of each generation, the chiefs of each generation, the presidents of academies of each generation, the magistrates of each generation, the princes of each generation, the counsellors of each generation, the nobles of each generation, and the men of might of each generation, the elders of each generation, and the guides of each generation.

(3) And I saw Adam, his generation, their doings and their thoughts,Noah and his generation, their doings and their thoughts, and the generation of the flood, their doings and their thoughts, Shem and his generation, their doings and their thoughts, Nimrod and the generation of the confusion of tongues, and his generation, their doings and their thoughts, Abraham and his generation, their doings and their thoughts, Isaac and his generation, their doings and their thoughts, Ishmael and his generation, their doings and their thoughts, Jacob and his generation, their doings and their thoughts, Joseph and his generation, their doings and their thoughts, the tribes and their generation, their doings and their thoughts, Amram and his generation, their doings and their thoughts, Moses and his generation, their doings and their thoughts,

(4) Aaron and Mirjam their works and their doings, the princes and the elders, their works and doings, Joshua and his generation, their works and

doings, the judges and their generation, their works and doings, Eli and his generation, their works and doings, "Phinehas, their works and doings, Elkanah and his generation, their works and their doings, Samuel and his generation, their works and doings, the kings of Judah with their generations, their works and their doings, the kings of Israel and their generations, their works and their doings, the princes of Israel, their works and their doings; the princes of the nations of the world, their works and their doings, the heads of the councils of Israel, their works and their doings ; the heads of (the councils in) the nations of the world, their generations, their works and their doings; the rulers of Israel and their generation, their works and their doings ; the nobles of Israel and their generation, their works and their doings ; the nobles of the nations of the world and their generation(s), their works and their doings; the men of reputation in Israel, their generation, their works and their doings ; the judges of Israel, their generation, their works and their doings ; the judges of the nations of the world and their generation, their works and their doings ; the teachers of children in Israel, their generations, their works and their doings ; the teachers of children in the nations of the world, their generations, their works and their doings; the counsellors (interpreters) of Israel, their generation, their works and their doings ; the counsellors (interpreters) of the nations of the world, their generation, their works and their doings ; all the prophets of Israel, their generation, their works and their do-ings ; all the prophets of the nations of the world, their generation, their works and their doings ;

(5) and all the fights and wars that the nations 16 of the world wrought against the people of Israel in the time of their kingdom. And I saw Messiah, son of Joseph, and his generation "and their" works and their doings that they will do against the nations of the world. And I saw Messiah, son of David, and his generation, and all the fights and wars, and their works and their doings that they will do with Israel both for good and evil. And I saw all the fights and wars that Gog and Magog will fight in the days of Messiah, and all that the Holy One, blessed be He, will do with them in the time to come.

(6) And all the rest of all the leaders of the generations and all the works of the generations both in Israel and in the nations of the world, both what is done and what will be done hereafter to all generations until the end of time, (all) were graven on the Curtain of MAQOM. And I saw all these things with my eyes; and after I had seen it, I opened my mouth in praise of MAQOM (the Divine Majesty) (saying thus, Eccl. viii. 4, 5): "For the King's word hath power (and who may say unto him: What doest thou?) Whoso keepeth the commandments shall know no evil thing". And I said: (Ps. civ. 24) "O Lord, how manifold are thy works!".

CHAPTER XLVI

The place of the stars shown to R. Ishmael

R. Ishmael said: Metatron said to me:

(1) (Come and I will show thee) the space of the stars a that are standing in Raqia' night by night in fear of the Almighty (MAQOM) and (I will show thee) where they go and where they stand.

(2) I walked by his side, and he took me by his hand and pointed out all to me with his fingers. And they were standing on sparks of flames round the Merkaba of the Almighty (MAQOM). What did Metatron do? At that moment he clapped his hands and chased them off from their place. Forthwith they flew off on flaming wings, rose and fled from the four sides of the Throne of the Merkaba, and (as they flew) he told me the names of every single one. As it is written (Ps. cxlvii. 4):" He telleth the number of the stars ; he giveth them all their names", teaching, that the Holy One, blessed be He, has given a name to each one of them.

(3) And they all enter in counted order under the guidance of (lit. through, by the hands of) RAHATIEL to Raqia' ha-shSHamayim to serve the world. And they go out in counted order to praise the Holy One, blessed be He, with songs and hymns, according as it is written (Ps. xix. i): "The heavens declare the glory of God".

(4) But in the time to come the Holy One, blessed be He, will create them anew, as it is written (Lam. iii. 23):

"They are new every morning". And they open their mouth and utter a song.

Which is the song that they utter? (Ps. viii. 3): "When I consider thy heavens".

CHAPTER XLVII

Metatron shows R. Ishmael the spirits of the punished angels

R. Ishmael said: Metatron said to me:

(1) Come and I will show thee the souls of the angels and the spirits of the ministering servants whose bodies have been burnt in the fire of MAQOM (the Almighty) that goes forth from his little finger. And they have been made into fiery coals in the midst of the fiery river (Nehar di-Nur). But their spirits and their souls are standing behind the Shekina.

(2) Whenever the ministering angels utter a song at a wrong timeor as not appointed to be sung they are burnt and consumed by the fire of their Creator and by a flame from their Maker, in the places (chambers) of the whirlwind, for it blows upon them and drives them into the Nehar di-Nur; and there they are made into numerous mountains of burning coal. But their spirit and their soul return to their Creator, and all are standing behind their Master.

(3) And I went by his side and he took me by his hand ; and he showed me all the souls of the angels and the spirits of the ministering servants who were standing behind the Shekina upon wings of the whirlwind and walls of fire surrounding them.

(4) At that moment Metatron opened to me the gates of the walls within which they were standing behind the Shekina, And I lifted up my eyes and saw them, and behold, the likeness of every one was as (that of) angels and their wings like birds' (wings), made out of flames, the work of burning fire. In that moment I opened my mouth in praise of MAQOM and said (Ps. xcii. 5):

"How great are thy works, O Lord ".

CHAPTER XLVIII (A)

Metatron shows R. Ishmael the Right Hand of the Most High, now inactive behind Him, but in the future destined to work the deliverance of Israel

R. Ishmael said: Metatron said to me:

(1) Come, and I will show thee the Right Hand of MAQOM, laid behind (Him) because of the destruction of the Holy Temple ; from which all kinds of splendour and light shine forth and by which the 955 heavens were created ; and whom not even the Seraphim and the 'Ophannim are permitted (to behold), until the day of salvation shall arrive.

(2) And I went by his side and he took me by his hand and showed me (the Right Hand of MAQOM), with all manner of praise, rejoicing and song: and no mouth can tell its praise, and no eye can behold it, because of its greatness, dignity, majesty, glory and beauty.

(3) And not only that, but all the souls of the righteous who are counted worthy to behold the joy of Jerusalem, they are standing by it, praising and praying before it three times every day, saying (Is.li.9): "Awake, awake, put on strength, O arm of the Lord" according as it is written (Is. lxiii. 12): "He caused his glorious arm to go at the right hand of Moses".

(4) In that moment the Right Hand of MAQOM was weeping. And there went forth from its five fingers five rivers of tears and fell down into the great sea and shook the whole world, according as it is written (Is. xxiv. 19, 20): "The earth is utterly broken (1), the earth is clean dissolved (2), the earth is moved exceedingly (3), the earth shall stagger like a drunken man (4) and shall be moved to and fro like a hut (5)", five times corresponding to the fingers of his Great Right Hand.

(5) But when the Holy One, blessed be He, sees, that there is no righteous man in the generation, and no pious man (Chasid] on earth, and no justice in the hands of men ; and (that there is) no man like unto Moses, and no intercessor as Samuel who could pray before MAQOM for the salvation and for the deliverance, and for His Kingdom, that it be revealed in the whole world; and for His great Right Hand that He put it before Himself again to work great salvation by it for Israel,

(6) then forthwith will the Holy One, blessed be He, remember His own justice, favour, mercy and grace: and He will deliver His great Arm by himself, and His righteousness will support Him. According as it is written (Is. lix.

16): "And he saw, that there was no man" (that is:) like unto Moses who prayed countless times for Israel in the desert and averted the (Divine) decrees from them" and he wondered, that there was no intercessor" like unto Samuel who intreated the Holy One, blessed be He, and called unto Him and he answered him and fulfilled his desire, even if it was not fit (in accordance with the Divine plan), according as it is written (i Sam. xii. 17): "Is it not wheat-harvest today? I will call unto the Lord".

(7) And not only that, but He joined fellowship with Moses in every place, as it is written (Ps.xcix.6): "Moses and Aaron among His priests." And again it is written (Jer. xv. i): "Though Moses and Samuel stood before me" (Is. lxiii. 5): "Mine own arm brought salvation unto me".

(8) Said the Holy One, blessed be He in that hour: " How long shall I wait for the children of men to work salvation according to their righteousness for my arm? For my own sake and for the sake of my merit and righteousness will I deliver my arm and by it redeem my children from among the nations of the world.

As it is written (Is. xlviii. n): "For my own sake will I do it. For how should my name be profaned".

(9) In that moment will the Holy One, blessed be He, reveal His Great Arm and show it to the nations of the world: for its length is as the length of the world and its breadth is as the width of the world. And the appearance of its splendour is like unto the splendour of the sunshine in its might, in the summer solstice.

(10) Forthwith Israel will be saved from among the nations of the world. And Messiah will appear unto them and He will bring them up to Jerusalem with great joy. And not only that but Israel will come from the four quarters of the World and eat with Messiah. But the nations of the world shall not eat with them, as it is written (Is. Hi. 10): "The Lord hath made bare his holy arm in the eyes of all the nations ; and all the ends of the earth shall see the salvation of our God". And again (Deut. xxxii. 12): "The Lord alone did lead him, and there was no strange god with him". (Zech. xiv. 9): "And the Lord shall be king over all the earth".

CHAPTER XLVIII (cont.) (B)

The Divine Names that go forth from the Throne of Glory, crowned and escorted by numerous angelic hosts through the heavens and back again to the Throne the angels sing the 'Holy' and the 'Blessed'

These are the seventy-two names written on the heart of the Holy One, blessed be He: SS, SeDeQ {righteousness), SaHPeL SUR {Is. xxvi. **4**}, SBI, SaDdlQ{righteous}, S'Ph, SHN, SeBa'oTh {Lord of Hosts},ShaDdaY {God Almighty}, 'eLoHIM {God}, YHWH, SH, DGUL, W'DOM, SSS", 'YW, 'F, 'HW, HB, YaH, HW, WWW, SSS, PPP, NN, HH, HaY {living}, HaY, ROKeB 'aRaBOTh {riding upon the 'Araboth', Ps. Ixviii. **5**}, YH, HH, WH, MMM, NNN, HWW, YH, YHH, HPhS, H'S, 'I, W, S", Z', "', QQQ {Holy, Holy, Holy}, QShR, BW, ZK,

GINUR, GINURYa', Y', YOD, 'aLePh, H'N, P'P, R'W, YYWy YYW, BBS, DDD, TTT, KKK, KLL, SYS, 'XT', BShKMLW {= blessed be the Name of His glorious kingdom for ever and ever}, completed for MeLeK HalOLaM {the King of the Universe], JBRH LB' {the beginning of Wisdom for the children of men}, BNLK W" Y {blessed be He who gives strength to the weary and increaseth strength to them that have no might, Is. xl. **29**}that go forth (adorned) with numerous crowns of fire with numerous crowns of flame, with numerous crowns of chashmal, with numerous crowns of lightning from before the Throne of Glory. And with them (there are) thousand hundreds of power (i.e. powerful angels) who escort them like a king with trembling and dread, with awe and shivering, with honour and majesty andfear, with terror, with greatness and dignity, with glory and strength, with understanding and knowledge and with a pillar of fire and a pillar of flame and lightning and their light is as lightnings of light and with the likeness of the chashmal.

(2) And they give glory unto them and they answer and cry before them: Holy, Holy, Holy.

And they roll (convoy) them through every heaven as mighty and honoured princes. And when they bring them all back to the place of the Throne of Glory, then all the Chayyoth by the Merkaba open their mouth in praise of His glorious name, saying: "Blessed be the name of His glorious kingdom for ever and ever".

CHAPTER XLVIII (cont.) (c)

An Enoch-Metatron piece

ALT 1

(1) "I seized him, and I took him and I appointed him" that is Enoch, the son of Jared, whose name is Metatron

(2) and I took him from among the children of men

(5) and made him a Throne over against my Throne. Which is the size of that Throne? Seventy thousand parasangs (all) of fire.

(9) I committed unto him 70 angels corresponding to the nations (of the world) and I gave into his charge all the household above and below.

(7) And I committed to him Wisdom and Intelligence more than (to) all the angels. And I called his name "the LESSER YAH", whose name is by Gematria 71. And I arranged for him all the works of Creation. And I made his power to transcend (lit. I made for him power more than) all the ministering angels.

ALT 2

(3) He committed unto Metatron that is Enoch, the son of Jared all treasuries. And I appointed him over all the stores that I have in every heaven. And I committed into his hands the keys of each heavenly store.

(4) I made (of) him the prince over all the princes, and I made (of) him a minister of my Throne of Glory, to provide for and arrange the Holy Chayyoth, to wreathe crowns for them (to crown them with crowns), to clothe them with honour and majesty to prepare for them a seat when he is sitting on his throne to magnify his glory in the height.

(5) The height of his stature among all those (that are) of high stature (is) seventy thousand parasangs. And I made his glory great as the majesty of my glory.

(6) and the brilliance of his eyes as the splendour of the Throne of Glory.

(7) his garment honour and majesty, his royal crown 500 by 500 parasangs.

ALT 3

(1) Aleph1 I made him strong, I took him, I appointed him: (namely) Metatron, my servant who is one (unique) among all the children of heaven. I made him strong in the generation of the first Adam. But when I beheld the men of the generation of the flood, that they were corrupt, then I went and removed my Shekina from among them. And I lifted it up on high with the sound of a trumpet and with a shout, as it is written (Ps.xlvii. 6): "God is gone up with a shout, the Lord with the sound of a trumpet".

(2) "And I took him": (that is) Enoch, the son of Jared, from among them. And I lifted him up with the sound of a trumpet and with a tera'a (shout) to the high heavens, to be my witness together with the Chayyoth by the Merkaba in the world to come.

(3) I appointed him over all the treasuries and stores that I have in every heaven. And I committed into his hand the keys of every several one.

(4) I made (of) him the prince over all the princes and a minister of the Throne of Glory (and) the Halls of 'Araboth: to open their doors to me, and (of) the Throne of Glory, to exalt an arrange it; (and I appointed him over) the Holy Chayyot to wreathe crowns upon their heads; the majestic 'Ophannim, to crown them with strength and glory; the; honoured Kerubim, to clothe: them in majesty; over the radiant sparks, to make them to shine with splendour and brilliance; over the flaming Seraphim, to cover them with highness; the Chashmallim of light, to make them radiant with Light and to prepare the seat for me every morning as I sit upon the Throne of Glory. And to extol and magnify my glory inthe height of my power; (and I have committed unto him) the secrets of above and the secrets of below (heavenly secrets and earthly secrets).

(5) I made him higher than all. The height of his stature, in the midst of all (who are) high of stature (I made) seventy thousand parasangs. I made his Throne great by the majesty of my Throne. And I increased its glory by the honour of my glory.

(6) I transformed his flesh into torches of fire, and all the bones of his body into fiery coals; and I made the appearance of his eyes as the lightning, and the light of his eyebrows as the imperishable light. I made his face bright as the splendour of the sun, and his eyes as the splendour of the Throne of Glory.

(7) I made honour and majesty his clothing, beauty and highness his covering cloak and a royal crown of 500 by (times) 500 parasangs (his) diadem. And I put upon him of my honour, my majesty and the splendour. of my glory that is upon my Throne of Glory. I called him the LESSER YHWH, the Prince of the Presence, the Knower of Secrets: for every secret did I reveal to him as a father and all mysteries declared I unto him in uprightness.

(8) I set up his throne at the door of my Hall that he may sit and judge the heavenly household on high. And I placed every prince before him, to receive authority from him, to perform his will.

(9) Seventy names did I take from (my) names and called him by them to enhance his glory.

Seventy princes gave I into his hand, to command unto them my precepts and my words in every language: to abase by his word the proud to the ground, and to exalt by the utterance of his lips the humble to the height ; to smite kings by his speech, to turn kings away from their paths, to set up(the) rulers over their dominion as it is written (Dan.ii. 21): "and he changeth the times and the seasons, and to give wisdom unto all the setwise of the world and understanding (and) knowledge to all who understand knowledge, as it is griten (Dan. ii. 21): " and knowledge to them that know understanding", to reveal to them the secrets of my words and to teach the decree of my righteous judgement,

(10) as it is written (Is.Iv. n): "so shall my word be that goeth forth out of my mouth; it shall not return unto me void but shall accomplish (that which I please)". 'E'eseh' (I shall accomplish) is not written here, but "asdh' (he shall accomplish), meaning, that whatever word and whatever utterance goes forth from before the Holy One, blessed be He, Metatron stands and carries it out. And he establishes the decrees of the Holy One, blessed be He.

CHAPTER XLVIII (D)

The names of Metatron. The treasuries of Wisdom opened to Moses on mount Sinai. The angels protest against Metatron for revealing the secrets to Moses and are answered and rebuked by God. The chain of tradition and the power of the transmitted mysteries to heal diseases

(1) Seventy names has Metatron which the Holy One, blessed be He, took from his own name and put upon him. And these they are:

YeHOEL, YaH, YeHOEL, YOPHIEL and Yophphiel, and 'APHPHIEL and MaRGeZIEL, GIPpUYEL, Pa'aZIEL, 'A'aH, PeRIEL, TaTRIEL, TaB-KIEL,'W, YHWH, DH, WHYH, 'eBeD, DiBbURIEL, 'aPh'aPIEL, SPPIEL, PaSPaSIEL, SeNeGRON, MeTaTRON, SOGDIN, 'ADRIGON, ASUM, SaQPaM, SaQTaM, MIGON MITTON, MOTTRON, ROSPHIM, QINOTh, ChaTaTYaH, DeGaZYaH, PSPYaH, BSKNYH, MZRG, BaRaD.., MKRKK, MSPRD, ChShG, ChShB, MNRTTT, BSYRYM, MITMON, TITMON, PiSQON,

SaPhSaPhYaH, ZRCh, ZRChYaH, B', BeYaH, HBH BeYaH, PeLeT, PLTYaH, RaBRaBYaH, ChaS, ChaSYaH, TaPhTaPhYaH, TaMTa-MYaH, SeHaSYaH, IRURYaH, 'aL'aLYaH, BaZRIDYaH, SaTSaT-KYaH, SaSDYaH, RaZRaZYAH, BaZRaZYaH, 'aRIMYaH, SBHYaH, SBIBKHYH, SiMKaM, YaHSeYaH, SSBIBYaH, SaBKaSBeYaH, QeLILQaLYaH, fKIHHH, HHYH, WH, WHYH, ZaKklKYaH, TUTRISYaH, SURYaH, ZeH, PeNIRHYaH, Z1Z'H, GaL Ra-ZaYYa, MaMLIKYaH, TTYaH, eMeQ, QaMYaH, MeKaPpeRYaH, PeRISHYaH, SePhaM, GBIR, GiB-bORYaH, GOR, GORYaH, ZIW, 'OKBaR, the LESSER YHWH, after the name of his Master, (Ex. xxiii. 21) "for my name is in him", RaBIBIEL, TUMIEL, Segansakkiel ('Sagnezagiel' / 'Neganzegael), the Prince of Wisdom.

(2) And why is he called by the name Sagnesakiel? Because all the treasuries of wisdom are committed in his hand.

(3) And all of them were opened to Moses on Sinai, so that he learnt them during the forty days, while he was standing (remaining}: the Torah in the seventy aspects of the seventy tongues, the Prophets in the seventy aspects of the seventy tongues, the Writings in the seventy aspects of the seventy tongues, "the Halakas in the seventy aspects of the seventy tongues, the Traditions in the seventy aspects of the seventy tongues, the Haggadas in the seventy aspects of the seventy tongues and the Toseftas in the seventy aspects of the seventy tongues'.

(4) But as soon as the forty days were ended, he forgot all of them in one moment. Then the Holy One, blessed be He, called Yephiphyah, the Prince of the Law, and (through him) they were given to Moses as a gift. As it is written (Deut. x. 4): "and the Lord gave them unto me". And after that it remained with him. And whence do we know, that it remained (in his memory) ? Because it is written (Mai. iv. 4): " Remember ye the Law of Moses my servant which I commanded unto him in Horeb for all Israel, even my statutes and judgements". The Law of Moses': that is the Tora, the Prophets and the Writings, 'statutes': that is the Halakas and Traditions, 'judgements'; that is the Haggadas and the Toseftas. And all of them were given to Moses on high on Sinai.

(5) These seventy names (are) a reflection of the Explicit Name(s) on the Merkaba which are graven upon the Throne of Glory. For the Holy One, blessed be He, took from His Explicit Name(s) and put upon the name of Metatron: Seventy Names of His by which the ministering angels call the King of the kings of kings, blessed be He, in the high heavens, and twenty-two letters that are on the ring upon his finger with which are sealed the destinies of the princes of kingdoms on high in greatness and power and with which are sealed the lots of the Angel of Death, and the destinies of every nation and tongue.

(6) Said Metatron, the Angel, the Prince of the Presence; the Angel, the Prince of the Wisdom; the Angel, the Prince of the Understanding; the Angel, the Prince of the Kings; the Angel, the Prince of the Rulers; the angel, the Prince of the Glory; the angel, the Prince of the high ones, and of the princes, the exalted, great and honoured ones, in heaven and on earth:

(7) "H, the God of Israel, is my witness in this thing, (that] when I revealed this secret to Moses, then all the hosts in every heaven on high raged against me and said to me:

(8) Why dost thou reveal this secret to son of man, born of woman, tainted and unclean, a man of a putrefying drop, the secret by which were created heaven and earth, the sea and the dry land, the mountains and hills, the rivers and springs, Gehenna of fire and hail, the Garden of Eden and the Tree of Life; and by which were formed Adam and Eve, and the cattle, and the wild beasts, and the fowl of the air, and the fish of the sea, and Behemoth and Leviathan, and the creeping things, the worms, the dragons of the sea, and the creeping things of the deserts; and the Tora and Wisdom and Knowledge and Thought and the Gnosis of things above and the fear of heaven. Why dost thou reveal this to flesh and blood? I answered them: Because the Holy One, blessed be He, has given me authority, And furthermore, I have obtained permission from the high and exalted Throne, from which all the Explicit Names go forth with lightnings of fire and flaming chashmallim.

(9) But they were not appeased, until the Holy One, blessed be He, rebuked

them and drove them away with rebuke from before him, saying to them:
"I delight in, and have set my love on,
and have entrusted and committed
unto Metatron, my Servant, alone, for
he is One (unique) among all the children of heaven.

(10) And Metatron brought them out
from his house of treasuries and committed them to Moses, and Moses to
Joshua, and Joshua to the elders, and
the elders to the prophets and the
prophets to the men of the Great Synagogue, and the men of the Great
Synagogue to Ezra and Ezra the
Scribe to Hillel the elder, and Hillel
the elder to R. Abbahu and R. Abbahu
to R. Zera, and R. Zera to the men of
faith, and the men of faith (committed
them) to give warning and to heal by
them all diseases that rage in the
world, as it is written (Ex. xv. 26): "If
thou wilt diligently hearken to the
voice of the Lord, thy God, and wilt do
that which is right in his eyes, and wilt
give ear to his commandments, and
keep all his statutes, I will put none of
the diseases upon thee, which I have
put upon the Egyptians: for I am the
Lord, that healeth thee".

(Ended and finished. Praise be unto
the Creator of the World.)

www.ingramcontent.com/pod-product-compliance
Lightning Source LLC
La Vergne TN
LVHW011201080426
835508LV00007B/536